Sheep

Animal

Series editor: Jonathan Burt

Sheep

Philip Armstrong

REAKTION BOOKS

For Annie

Published by
REAKTION BOOKS LTD
Unit 32, Waterside
44–48 Wharf Road
London N1 7UX, UK
www.reaktionbooks.co.uk

First published 2016, reprinted 2017
Copyright © Philip Armstrong 2016

Printed and bound in China by 1010 Printing International Ltd

A catalogue record for this book is available from the British Library

ISBN 978 1 78023 593 6

Contents

1 Sheepishness

The sheep approaches to see if I have anything to offer. I try to read his face, but it's difficult: the eyes all but disappear behind the big searching muzzle. When at last his gaze meets mine, I find it off-putting. The pupils aren't circular like a human's, but slits. Nor are they vertical like a cat's eyes. They are more alien than that: horizontal slots across a pale yellow cornea. In the face of the goat standing next to us, between the horns rising from the top of his head and the beard dangling from his chin, those sideways eyes seem full of diabolical intelligence and character. But the sheep's face, between long ears that poke horizontally from the side of the head, and a beardless chin overshot by a broad nose, is all laterals and no verticals, so the sideways shape of his pupils is exaggerated rather than complemented. If this sheep's face was a hospital monitor, it would be flatlining: no sign of life.

Sheep are hard to read.

Partly this is because they are so familiar. Along with their closest relatives, goats, sheep have been an intimate part of human lives for 11,000 years – longer than any other species except the dog. Our landscapes are full of them, and our houses and wardrobes and refrigerators are full of what we make of them – as are our churches, sacred scriptures, books, visual arts and popular culture. Millennia spent making sheep into what we want them

Ruminating sheep.

The spring lamb has been a common motif of New Zealand postcards for decades.

to be – both in the flesh, and in our collective imaginations – obscures our view of what they really are, in themselves.

It is this paradox that has brought me to a farm animal sanctuary to meet a couple of sheep in person. I live in a country whose modern economy, society and landscape have all been shaped by sheep-farming more than by any other single force – a country in which, during my childhood, there were 30 sheep for every human being. Yet I had never, before this day, spent any time with actual live sheep – never touched one. Even in my country, in which sheep are everywhere, they are nevertheless for most of us, most of the time, out of the way.

I grew up in New Zealand in the 1970s, a decade in which the number of sheep in the country rose to its all-time high of 70 million. Along with everything else it gave us (including an economy), the national flock provided the standard caricature of New Zealand to a world ignorant of any other fact about the place. Given the extent to which settler New Zealand was built on the wool and meat of *Ovis aries*, it is hard to argue that the joke was unfair. The most common postcard available to overseas tourists,

8

the one designed to epitomize our country, showed spring lambs and daffodils. Most likely, those adorable baby animals ended up on a family dinner table as roast legs of lamb, the meal that came closest to a national dish. To grow up as I did was to experience a world that was more sheep-shaped than any other before or since.

Yet readers of this book will also belong to cultures that have been formed, to some degree and in certain ways, by the lives and deaths of sheep. New Zealand is only one legatee, albeit a conspicuous one, of *Homo sapiens*'s long-standing engagement with *Ovis*. Somewhere around 9000 BCE, sheep were domesticated by humans. And from these flocks came the cultural phenomena that constitute civilization as we commonly understand it: cities, religion, writing, accounting, commerce, capital, industry.

At the same time, we have exploited the bodies of sheep for material purposes – fleecing them, so to speak, of their fibre and flesh, their milk and their mammary cells. We have also made profligate use of them as signifiers, as bearers of our meanings. In this respect *Ovis aries* epitomizes Henry David Thoreau's insight that, for humans, animals 'are all beasts of burden, in a sense, made to carry some portion of our thoughts'.[1] In the case of sheep this has been literally true: until the importation of papermaking techniques from China during the Middle Ages, European books and documents were inscribed on parchment made from animal hides, predominantly those of sheep.

Of course, we have made extensive – indeed unlimited – use of many other species as well. Yet no other domestic animal fades from view, even as we use it, quite as completely as the sheep. No other animal tends so thoroughly to become (for most of us) nothing *but* a signifier or blank page or resource unit. For it is surely the case that, despite their massive contribution to our lives – past and present – we think less of sheep than just about any other animal. This is the species we make proverbial for stupidity and failure to stand out from the crowd. To be or behave like a (flock of) sheep means to give up one's individualism, identity, initiative, intelligence and will. Even our word for them (in English) fails to distinguish between the singular and the plural. It's no surprise that in George Orwell's political fable *Animal Farm* (1945), for instance, it is the sheep who accept indoctrination by the ruling pigs most easily, and whose brainwashed chorus of 'Four legs good, two legs bad' is used to silence any opposition or resistance.[2]

Where do they come from, these stereotypes that portray sheep as the most negligible, the most easily dismissed, the most routinely overwritten of animals? As we examine the history of our species's attitude to sheep, we find that even the ways in which we habitually dismiss them have much to tell us.

The presumption that sheep are unintelligent can be found as far back as Aristotle, who asserted in about 350 BCE that

> the sheep is said to be naturally dull and stupid. Of all quadrupeds it is the most foolish: it will saunter away to lonely places with no object in view; oftentimes in stormy weather it will stray from shelter.

Yet just a couple of paragraphs later, he remarks that 'shepherds train sheep to close in together at a clap of their hands', so that 'when a thunderstorm comes on', they can summon their flocks back to the sheepfold.[3] The contradictions here resound throughout history: sheep are stupid because they follow obediently, but also because they stray disobediently; they are too dull to know what they are doing, but they can learn to come on command (like dogs, in whom we consider this to be evidence of human-like cleverness).

From Shakespeare's day comes the most charming expression of the already ancient belief in ovine silliness: Edward Topsell in his *History of Four-footed Beasts* (1607) concedes with regret that 'the head of the sheep is very weak, and his braine not fat.'[4] Less charmingly, a century and half later, during the era of the great systematizers of the Enlightenment, the pre-eminent French naturalist Georges-Louis Leclerc, Comte de Buffon, considered 'the weakness and stupidity of the sheep' to be so extreme that 'without the assistance of man, the sheep could never have subsisted, or continued its species in a wild state.' Fortunately, it so happens that 'this animal, so contemptible in itself, and so devoid of every mental quality, is, of all others, the most extensively useful to man.'[5] Here is another formula central to the human–ovine relationship: the sheer inanity of sheep justifies our use of them.

A further variation on the theme of sheepish dimness is demonstrated in the following century, and on the other side of the world, by Lady Mary Anne Barker, a well-to-do settler in colonial New Zealand. In her book *Station Amusements* (1873), designed to entertain a London readership with tales of life on an antipodean sheep run, Barker introduces a chapter entitled 'Our Pets' by distinguishing between dogs, cats, horses and fowl, all of who possess 'individuality', the capacity necessary for them to be companions of humans, and sheep, who do not:

> I never heard [sheep] spoken of with affection . . . This must surely arise from their enormous numbers. 'How can you be fond of thousands of anything?' said a shepherd once to me, in answer to some sentimental inquiry of mine respecting his feelings towards his flock. That is the fact. There were too many sheep in our 'happy Arcadia' for any body to value or pet them . . . Even the touching patience of

Explano supscpte hystorie.   cia unu corpus. Regnab't usq:

the poor animals beneath the shears, or amid the dust and noise of the yards, was generally despised as stupidity.[6]

Two further important and durable themes emerge here. First, sheep can only be conceived as a mass of identical units rather than individuals. Second, their 'patience', in the old sense of acceptance of suffering, is 'despised as stupidity'.

This latter stereotype, that of the sheep as long-suffering or self-surrendering, has its own powerful cultural genealogy – and one that, most paradoxically, derives from a symbolic status more exalted, potent and central than any other creature in Western culture. For within the Christian tradition, the sheep – or more specifically the lamb – stands for Jesus Christ himself.

The sheep appears at the very origins of the Jewish and Christian Old Testament traditions, identified from the outset as the archetypal sacrificial victim and the incarnation of passive surrender. In Genesis the first animal sacrifice occurs when the shepherd Abel, son of Adam and Eve, offers to God the 'firstlings of his flock' (Genesis 4:4). The original 'scapegoat' is actually a sheep: God provides Abraham with 'a ram caught in a thicket by his horns' as a substitute victim for his son Isaac (Genesis 22:13). Lambs, in particular, remain stuck with this role throughout the scriptures. Examples include the Passover lambs' blood that preserves the Israelites from the death of the firstborn in Egypt, and the proverbially meek and self-sacrificing 'lamb to the slaughter' foreseen by the prophet Isaiah, who, 'as a sheep before her shearers is dumb . . . openeth not his mouth' (53:7). These archetypes are taken up in the New Testament, where Jesus becomes 'the Lamb of God, which taketh away the sin of the world' (John 1:19). In the Book of Revelation, the 'Lamb that was slain' appears as one of the apocalyptic manifestations of Christ (5:8). Despite this particular Lamb's assertive actions – he presides over the

Christ as the 'Little Lamb' defeating the ten kings: illustration to Beatus of Liébana's *Commentary on the Apocalypse,* c. 1220–35.

destruction of the heavens and the earth – the Greek word used is not the usual *amnos*, 'lamb', but the diminutive *arnion*, 'little lamb', or 'lambkin'.

The imagery of the shepherd and his flock is also repeated frequently in both Testaments, where it provides the symbol of the submission of God's people to his will: the Psalmist sings, 'he is our God; and we are the people of his pasture, and the sheep of his hand' (95:7), while St John writes, 'he goeth before them, and the sheep follow him: for they know his voice' (10:4). In Christian tradition, the sheep remained the epitome and emblem of obedience to the will of God. The medieval bestiarists – writing most often on sheepskin parchment – described *Ovis* as 'a soft

Edward Burne-Jones,
The Good Shepherd,
1857, watercolour.

Four stamps issued
by New Zealand
Post for 2015, the
Chinese Year of the
Sheep.

Year of the Sheep
2015
$2.00
New Zealand

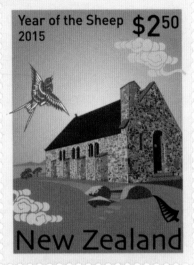

Year of the Sheep
2015
$2.50
New Zealand

Year of the Sheep
2015
80c
New Zealand

Year of the Sheep
2015
$1.40
New Zealand

Christ bequeathing his shepherd's crook to the clergy. Frontispiece to Hugo de Fouilloy, *Treatise on Shepherds and Flocks*, c. 1270.

animal with wool, a defenceless body, and a peaceful nature', who 'represent[s] the innocent and simple among Christians'.[7]

It is, then, to Judaeo-Christian thought that we owe the overwhelming Western association of sheepishness with self-abnegating passivity, an association so deeply engrained that it remains in force well beyond its religious origins. In today's secular cultures, this archetype of sheepish passivity, separated

Zhao Mengfu, *Sheep and Goat*, handscroll, Yuan Dynasty, China (1271–1368), ink on paper.

from its scriptural context, loses the original sense of redemptive self-surrender and folds back into the pre-existing (agricultural) idea of sheepish stupidity.

The exceptional power of these combined stereotypes becomes all the more striking if we compare them with other cultures' attitudes to *Ovis*, for the ascription of passivity and stupidity to sheep is a uniquely Western convention. In ancient China, for example, although sacrificing animals to ancestors was a fundamental part of religious practice, and references to the sacrifice of domesticated sheep can be found as far back as the Shang Dynasty (over 3,000 years ago), *Ovis* functioned merely as one sacrificial animal among others, rather than the paradigmatic one.[8] Nor does the Chinese tradition associate sheep strongly with surrender. The same word (*yáng*) applies to both sheep and goat, and since this is also the word for the masculine principle in nature (within the fundamental opposition of *yíng* and *yáng*) and for the sun, the image of the sheep/goat/ram signifies (from the Han dynasty onwards) auspiciousness, good fortune, 'renewal and change', 'happiness and prosperity'. Rams' heads were commonly used as a motif on roofing tiles, for example, to render the dwelling lucky. The eighth sign of the Chinese zodiac is either the goat or the sheep, and those born under that sign are, although

Petroglyphs of
bighorn sheep,
Moab, Utah, USA.

mainly placid and gentle by nature, also stubborn, strong-willed,
passionate and capable of militancy.[9]

In the Americas, by contrast with both the Chinese and
European traditions, familiarity with the indigenous sheep, the
perennially wild and indocible bighorn (*Ovis canadensis*), produced (for example, among the Hopi and Navajo) an association
of sheep with sharpness of sight and hearing, and with power
over nature and the body.[10]

Even in the so-called West the ancient and still-dominant
archetypes and stereotypes that associate sheep with mindless
lack of individuality have been challenged in recent years. Scientific
studies (discussed in detail in the next chapter) show that sheep
possess extensive spatial memories, ample capacity to learn from
experience and a highly developed ability (beyond that of dogs,
and comparable to humans' own) to identify individuals by their
faces, even after long periods of separation.

The chapters that follow are driven by these contradictions
between our commonest assumptions about sheep and the ways
in which the animals themselves challenge, subvert or resist

those assumptions – driven, so to speak, by the tension between sheepishness and sheepliness.

In writing this book, I have been repeatedly astonished by sheep. My more surprising discoveries include the following: the first domestic sheep were suckled rather than milked by humans; there have been sheep the size of oxen; ancient Romans and Greeks dressed their sheep in custom-made jackets; in Africa and Central Asia, rams sometimes wear aprons as a contraceptive measure; in parts of France, sheep have been shepherded on stilts; the catastrophic foot-and-mouth disease is no more dangerous to sheep than the common cold; the first cloned animal was a sheep; bighorn rams are mostly homosexual; sheep can recognize each other by their footprints; they can belch silently through their noses; they can see behind them without turning their heads; there are sheep with tails so fat they account for one-sixth of their total weight; there are sheep with four horns or six, and even with three or five.

(Actually, one item in the above list is false; by the end of this book the reader should know which. And here's a hint: it's not the most implausible one.)

Anti-mating aprons are still used to control unwanted breeding in flocks where ewes and rams cannot be separated.

Jean-Louis Gintrac, *Inhabitants of the Landes*, c. 1850, oil on canvas. French shepherds in the marshy Landes region used stilts to watch their flocks.

2 How Sheep Became

Most human cultures are well supplied with animal creation stories. The earliest-known literature, which the Sumerians inscribed on clay tablets over 4,000 years ago, includes a story about the gods' decision to create sheep and grain in order to raise humans out of their previous animal-like existence by supplying them with milk, oils, leather, yarns and textiles.[1]

Of course, creation myths like this don't tell us the facts about the origins of things. Rather, they explain how things are now by inventing an explanatory narrative for how they came to be. Rudyard Kipling coined the phrase 'Just So Stories', in the title he gave to a collection of children's tales published in 1902, to refer to this kind of narrative: 'How the Camel Got His Hump', 'How the Rhinoceros Got His Skin', 'How the Leopard Got His Spots', and so on. The penultimate story, 'The Cat that Walked by Himself', narrates the origins of domestication and civilization, which are achieved by Woman, but through her use of Sheep. Woman cooks a wild sheep and then uses the shoulder bone, the 'big-fat blade-bone' inscribed with 'wonderful marks', to create magic songs that enable her to tame Dog, Horse and Cow.[2]

Today the most compelling origin stories about animals are supplied by science. While these are the stories that provide the argument of this chapter, its title is chosen to remind the reader that even scientific accounts contain elements of the Just So story.

The main difference, of course, is that scientific explanations rely on fossil and genetic evidence, which is assessed according to empirical methods ranging from radiocarbon dating through to DNA analysis. Yet it can be too easy to forget that conclusions about such evidence necessarily include elements of interpretation and an overlay of narrative construction – and, as in the Just So story, these creative elements tend to be shaped by present-day concerns and values. That is why even evolutionary stories change over time and according to different accounts by different scientists. Ironically, it is when we forget that our scientific narratives are inevitably pervaded by story-making structures that we fail to assess them critically and instead come to accept them as simple truths. Thus they become our new creation myths, and we are back in the realm of faith, not science.

Some 2.5 million years ago in Eurasia, during the early Pleistocene, there lived the first sheep, which were as big as oxen. Or so the tale goes. M. L. Ryder, in his monumental book *Sheep and Man* (1983), no sooner makes this claim than he offers

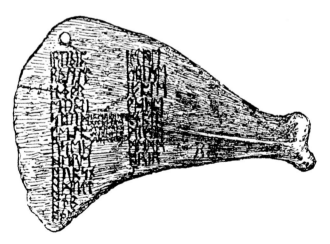

The 'big-fat blade-bone' from a shoulder of mutton, as drawn by Rudyard Kipling to illustrate his Just So story 'The Cat that Walked by Himself' (1902).

a qualification strong enough to turn it into little more than a likely story: 'the evolutionary sequence is poorly understood', he warns, because it occurred in mountains where erosion and glaciation tended to destroy fossil remains. All the same, he feels confident enough to assert – albeit in somewhat mythopoetic tones – that by the end of the Pleistocene, 'true sheep' had appeared and 'completely replaced the giants by the end of the ice ages'.[3]

Conflicting stories are also told about the relationships and distinctions among these hoofed pioneers. Most taxonomists recognize five species of sheep. Four are wild: the argali (*Ovis ammon*), the bighorn (*O. canadensis*), the urial (*O. vignei*) and the mouflon (*O. orientalis*). The fifth species is of course the ubiquitous domestic sheep (*O. aries*). Two other wild species commonly called sheep – the Barbary sheep (*Ammotragus lervia*), native to the rocky mountains of North Africa, and the blue sheep (*Pseudois nayaur*), which lives in the mountains of Tibet, Bhutan and western China – are, in fact, not sheep at all, but members of the goat-antelope family.[4]

The argali is the largest of the wild sheep types. Once widespread in Central and South Asia, *O. ammon* is now endangered as a result of habitat lost to pastures for its domestic relative, *O. aries*.[5] A subspecies, the Marco Polo sheep (*O. ammon polii*), is named after the thirteenth-century Venetian trader because he described them in his account of his journey through Central Asia. More than anything, Polo was astonished by their horns, which 'grow to as much as six palms in length and are never less than three or four', and from which 'the shepherds make big bowls from which they feed, and also fences to keep in their flocks'.[6] Further west, in Iran, Kazakhstan and parts of Pakistan and India, the argali gives way to the slightly smaller urial, also known as the arkars or shapo, which is the most elegantly attired

of the wild sheep types. Males wear a black ruff stretching from neck to chest, and both males and females have long, reddish-brown fleece that changes to a paler shade in winter.[7] The smallest of the wild sheep, the mouflon, is found today only in the Caucasus Mountains and in northern Iraq and Iran – and, in a variant endemic population, on the island of Cyprus, where it must have been introduced by humans as a domestic stock that subsequently went feral. Today, while its (supposed) descendants, the domestic *O. aries*, number more than a billion, the mouflon itself is endangered.[8] Ironically, when in 2001 scientists successfully created a viable clone of an endangered 'wild' species for the first time, they did so by producing a mouflon lamb.[9]

The bighorn of the Americas is more solidly built than the three Eurasian wild sheep types. *O. canadensis* has a broad chest,

A flock of urials resting on a hot day.

heavily muscled shoulders and haunches and shorter legs than its Old World cousins. Variations include the Alaskan Dall sheep, which is often pure white, and Stone sheep, which can be glossy black.[10]

However, things are rather more complicated than the above taxonomy implies. The commonest biological criterion for species differentiation is that animals from separate species cannot interbreed and produce fertile offspring: this is what sorts the sheep from the goats, for example, or the chimpanzees from humans. However, sheep trample happily (or hornily) across attempts to categorize them definitively, demonstrating that species and taxonomic classifications contain a large element of human artifice – because it turns out that all five 'species' of sheep can interbreed enthusiastically and successfully, which really, as Ryder comments

Mouflon rams in a defensive formation.

in his opening paragraph, 'implies that there is only one species'.[11] The differentiation of sheep into species, then, has less to do with biological reality than with human boundary-making.[12]

The story of sheep domestication – the creation of *O. aries* – is also a collection of shifting and contradictory narratives. Charles Darwin wrote in 1875 that 'most authors look at our domestic sheep as descended from several distinct species.' But then, having cited the arguments among experts regarding the number of distinct wild species, and their potential contributions to the lineage of *O. aries*, he concluded that the whole question of sheep ancestry remains in 'a hopeless state of doubt'.[13] In the early twentieth century J. C. Ewart attempted to resolve the conundrum by analysing skeletal remains from Neolithic sites in Switzerland and comparing them with the still-existing Soay sheep of Scotland's St Kilda archipelago, which are generally believed to be the most primitive surviving breed. He concluded that the urial and mouflon provided the foremothers and forefathers of *O. aries*.[14]

The subsequent advent of chromosomal studies threw this apparently simple conclusion back into doubt. Since the urial and the argali have different numbers of chromosomes (56 and 58 respectively) from both the mouflon and domestic sheep (both of which have 54), it would seem unlikely that any but the mouflon could have featured in the *O. aries* family tree. On the other hand, hybridization studies in the 1970s demonstrated that it would be possible for domestic sheep to have had some ancestors with higher chromosome numbers, which were subsequently selected

Part of a marble sarcophagus lid depicting Christ's separation of sheep from goats at the Last Judgement, c. 300 CE.

out of the gene pool. Meanwhile, studies of haemoglobin types possessed by *O. aries* but absent from all the currently existing wild sheep types led some experts to rule out even the long-standing favourite, the mouflon, as the chosen ancestor, and to conclude that domestic sheep must derive from one or more mystery species that are now extinct.[15] Which would seem to return us, after a century of hard work, to Darwin's shrug of hopeless doubt. In fact, though, most experts still consider the mouflon to be the likely ancestor, while conceding that it is possible that the domestic sheep may be the descendent instead of the urial; or of the urial and mouflon combined; or of neither of these, but instead of one or more extinct wild types; or of some other combination of the above. Such is the generosity of science as a generator of Just So stories.

More certainty attaches to the question of when and where and how *Ovis aries* emerged. The first clear evidence of domesticated sheep dates from about 9000 BCE, in northeastern Iraq; the first evidence in Europe comes from Greece in about 7200 BCE. However, as Ryder points out, since domestication is a very gradual process, a form of 'game management' of wild sheep must have occurred for a long time prior to these dates. From the outset, the domestic sheep was, as today, closely associated both with the goat and with pasturage. *Ovis* and *Capra* (goat) seem to have been domesticated at the same time, and often together, while crop farming appears to be a contemporaneous and closely related development.[16]

There are several aspects of the domestication of the sheep that might confound our assumptions. First, sheep were not initially domesticated for their meat or wool, but for their milk. The larger and more dangerous aurochs would not be transformed into docile and milk-yielding cattle for another two millennia, so sheep and goats provided the first source of animal milk for prehistoric human societies.[17] To use animals in this way makes better economic sense than raising them for meat: it takes far more energy, land and water for humans to produce feed for animals than it does to derive nourishment directly from crops, so a milk-producing animal delivers on that expensive investment better than one killed for meat. As a result, domestication at first led to a decline rather than an increase in meat consumption.[18]

But thinking carefully about the initial domestication of sheep actually yields even more surprising and counter-intuitive conclusions than this. Wild sheep are extremely wary, alert, fleet of foot and well equipped with defensive weaponry. How could such animals ever be induced, in the first instance, to accept the close contact and handling entailed by domestication? The most plausible explanation is that the initial taming depended on the process that behavioural scientists call 'imprinting': the establishment in baby animals of a close emotional dependence on human beings in place of their mothers. In such a predator-wary animal as *Ovis*, imprinting would need to occur very early in the lamb's life, certainly before weaning. And, prior to the domestication of other species, the only source of the milk needed for such young animals to survive to adulthood would have been human mothers. Accordingly, domestication of sheep most likely began with young women who adopted and nursed newborn orphan lambs – just as piglets are suckled in some cultures today.[19]

This conclusion, of course, overturns a number of our most durable origin stories about ourselves, which have tended to identify the origins of civilization in activities conventionally associated with masculinity, especially with hunting, and the development of tools and techniques for hunting and warfare.[20] By contrast, the story of *O. aries* suggests, as Ryder puts it, that it was 'not man the hunter, but woman in the home [who] had the most important

Spinning wool through the ages: a detail from an ancient Greek wine jug (*c.* 490 BCE) shows a drop spindle used to spin fibres from the distaff in the left hand.

role in domestication. Once the domestication of sheep and goats had been accomplished, their milk would have been available to assist the domestication of other species.'[21] (Curiously enough, this hypothesis echoes Rudyard Kipling's Just So story about domestication.)

As an explanation for domestication, the 'woman the nurturer' hypothesis has been slow to achieve recognition, no doubt precisely because it challenges some of the taken-for-granted beliefs that are served by other narratives about how both human and sheep came to be. It reminds us, perhaps uncomfortably, of the intimacy and mutuality of our kinship with animals. It puts life-nurturing women, rather than death-dealing men, at the heart of a process associated with the origins of 'Western civilization'. And it re-inserts intimate feelings of compassion into the very origins of an interaction – between ourselves and the animals we farm – that we usually find easier to understand in coldly rational terms. What would happen if, every time we passed a stock-truck full of sheep, or contemplated a leg of lamb, we thought about the nursing mother and lamb who began it all?

Whatever emotional bond may have been at work in the inaugural impulse that led to domestication, exploitation and killing followed soon enough. Once flocks of tame sheep were established to supply milk to humans rather than requiring it from them, most of the male lambs would have been killed for meat after they outgrew their usefulness in helping keep the ewes' milk flowing. Over time, such killing would have led to the observation that successive generations could be altered by choosing which rams to keep as sires. It is this artificial selection for traits desirable to humans that resulted in the major changes that today separate *O. aries* from wild species, which were all achieved in the first few thousand years of domestication – that is, by about 3000 BCE in Mesopotamia: a decrease in height and horn size, a lengthening of the tail and the development of a white fleece that grows continuously rather than undergoing an annual moult.[22] A critical part of this long process, of course, was the discovery of the extraordinary usefulness of wool, the attribute that made the sheep a more versatile stock animal than any other. Changes to the disposition of the animal were also brought about by the killing, by human breeders, of the more aggressive

A hand-tinted photograph of a man in Ramallah, 1919.

and recalcitrant, and perhaps also the cleverer, individuals. So it is that, in comparison with their wild cousins, domestic sheep have a smaller brain capacity, reduced visual acuity, smaller hearts and a lower production of adrenocortical steroid hormones – all of which suggest an increase in docility and a decrease in the animals' alertness.[23]

A drop spindle shown in William-Adolphe Bouguereau's *The Spinner*, 1873, oil on canvas.

The rest of this story – the development of the many breeds of domestic sheep, and of the historical relationship between humans and *O. aries* – belongs to the next three chapters. But first, having surveyed the various creation stories told by experts, we need to think about what it is, in biological terms, that makes a sheep a sheep.

According to taxonomists, *Ovis* belongs to the Bovidae family (along with bison, oxen, antelopes, goats and domestic cattle): herbivorous mammals with cloven hooves (unlike horses) and unbranched, permanent horns (as distinct from the antlers of deer, for example, which are shed seasonally). All bovids are ruminants: they have a system of multiple stomachs that allows them to regurgitate vegetation they have already partially digested in order to grind it up again with their teeth – in other words, they 'chew the cud'. This facilitates the slow fermentation of cellulose in the chamber of the four-part stomach called the 'rumen', which enables nutrition to be derived from heavily fibrous vegetable matter.[24] Rumination, however, takes time. Sheep have to spend about ten hours in every 24 grazing, and the same amount chewing cud. Accordingly they almost never sleep, at least not in the way that we do: 'If they sleep at all, the sleep must be only light and transient. This peculiarity is associated with the need to keep the head upright for regurgitation and belching during rumination.'[25] (It seems ironic, in this respect, that we speak of counting sheep as an aid to sleep.)

The apparently sardonic expression of a masticating sheep – the lower jaw moving from side to side, like a gangster chewing gum – is also part of the system of rumination. The grass is cropped by canines and incisors in the lower jaw, biting against a hard pad in the upper jaw (which has no front teeth), but it is the back teeth, ground together laterally, one side at a time, that break down the fresh grass and later the cud.[26]

Sheep can be distinguished from cattle – apart from being smaller in size than most cattle species – by the higher carriage of their heads and their narrow and hairy (rather than broad, naked and moist) muzzles, and their cleft upper lips. They differ from their closest relatives, goats, by being beardless, having tails that hang rather than stand erect, and possessing (usually) thicker horns that curve out from the side of the head rather than rising vertically from the top. These anatomical distinctions may not sound very significant, but they are outward manifestations of genetic differences sufficiently great that sheep and goats (usually) cannot interbreed successfully. And there is another trait that relates very closely to a key aspect of the sheep's psychological and social character: like some other bovids, but unlike goats, sheep have foot glands between their hooves. By this means they leave their scent on the ground as they trot – signing their names on the earth, as it were, wherever they go. These personal scent-trails are crucial to maintaining the bonds between flock members, and particularly the bond that holds ovine society together – that between lamb and ewe.[27]

There remains, of course, one more feature unique to sheep, an extraordinary adaptation that not only distinguishes *Ovis* from their closest relatives, but makes the species exceptionally useful to humans. This, of course, is wool.[28] Containing more than a hundred different proteins and two dozen different amino acids, wool is a highly complex substance. Each fibre grows in three layers. The outermost, the cuticle, takes the form of plates held together by a sort of protein glue and insulated by lanolin, a unique oily substance. (When wool is scoured – that is, cleaned in preparation for use by humans – the lanolin that has been removed is purified and used extensively in lubricants, adhesives, inks and cosmetics.) The two inner layers of the fibre are called the para-cortex and ortocortex, which grow together but asymmetrically,

The sardonic faces of cud-chewing sheep.

producing the crimp when wool becomes wet. Because of its layering and crimp, and its capacity to trap air between fibres, wool is an exceptionally effective insulator against the cold. In wet conditions, its thermal properties are even better: because the fibres are hydrophilic (they absorb water) without being hollow, they do not become waterlogged, but instead hold a supply of water that, warmed by the animal's body heat, becomes a further insulating layer. Meanwhile, wet wool actually produces chemicals that increase its temperature. Other properties – for example, the tiny pores that admit the passage of air in the surface layer – mean that wool also acts as a protector against excessive heat.[29] It is this remarkable versatility in their coats that enabled prehistoric sheep to follow the retreating glaciers and spread throughout Eurasia and the Americas, just as today it allows *Ovis* to thrive easily in habitats as hot as deserts and as cold as mountaintops, in the snows of Scandinavia and Scotland and the outback of Australia. And it is these same properties that made sheep central to the history of many human societies.

A sheeply attribute far less helpful to humans – which has therefore been reduced or eliminated in most domestic breeds – is the possession of large and powerful horns. Ryder identifies three important functions for horns in wild sheep. Most obviously, they are used 'for fighting, in which they serve as weapons, shields and shock absorbers'. In addition, being able to throw such a heavy mass of bony matter back and forth with a toss of the head is a considerable advantage when balancing on rocky slopes: in wild sheep the horns may constitute as much as 8 per cent of the live weight of the adult – as much as the rest of the skeleton in total. Finally, but not inconsequentially, horns may also assist in heat regulation: Ryder remarks that 'it is surprising how warm a horn often feels when one is handling sheep.'[30]

As the most spectacular feature of *Ovis* in their natural state – growing up to 190 cm (75 in.) in length (albeit coiled) and 50 cm (20 in.) in basal circumference – horns have tended to dominate

Diagram of wool fibre structure.

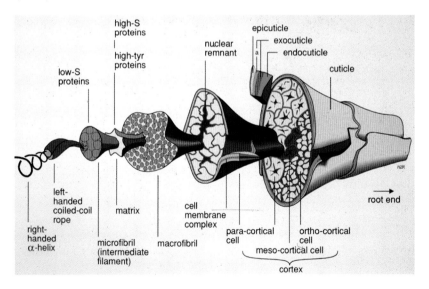

human perception of wild sheep, as the American name 'bighorn' exemplifies. In the standard ethological and evolutionary work on this species, Valerius Geist identifies horn size as the key to understanding *O. canadensis*. 'Leadership among rams is closely related to horn size', he asserts: 'the larger a ram's horns the more bands follow him, the larger the bands he leads, and hence the more sheep follow him.' Accordingly, he declares that 'breeding success run[s] parallel with horn size' as well.[31]

To be sure, it is hard not to be overawed observing fighting between bighorns, which is a spectacular display of balletic agility combined with bone-shuddering brute force. Each animal hurls its forequarters high in the air and then, while falling, throws one horn downwards to maximize the force of the impact. I have never seen a clash in real life, but video footage is sufficient to make me hold my breath in anticipation of the collision. Such fights seem to epitomize, then, the 'survival of the fittest' version of natural selection, which is encoded in Geist's simple formula: bigger horns = higher rank = greater success in breeding.

Yet, on closer inspection, this formula doesn't add up. For one thing, he tells us that although fighting among wild sheep is 'surprisingly common', actual bloodshed is rare, as are broken horns. Moreover, 'most of the fighting is initiated by the subordinate and executed in a manner harmless to the dominant'; that is, the animal with the smaller horns starts the fight. And both antagonists avoid aiming for body parts on which they could inflict real damage (as they would when fighting a predator, for instance). Rather they aim invariably for the shields provided by each other's horns, which makes clashes in wild rams seem rather less like the kind of armed combat described by Geist and others, and more like professional wrestling. Certainly most clashes seem designed not only to avoid causing real harm but even to avoid seriously challenging the existing hierarchy. This surely makes them rather irrelevant to the process of evolution through sexual selection, which requires genuine competition for the best mate. In addition, Geist tells us as an aside that 'females fight just like rams', even though they 'carry only tiny horns' – a phenomenon he does not try to explain.[32]

Subsequent studies of other kinds of free-living sheep contradict Geist's simplistic formula even more than some of his own observations: T. E. Rowell and C. A. Rowell, in an influential study of feral *O. aries*, found that the outright absence of horns did have some effect on rams' breeding success, but that 'there were no simple rules of interaction among rams based on horn size, nor indeed on any other aspect of appearance, nor on body weight'. In fact, this study goes on to point out that during clashes rams take great care to make impact with the base of the horn, the area of strong new growth, since the older horn further out is relatively weak. What matters in fighting is therefore strength

Bighorn rams clashing in the Rocky Mountains.

and size at the base of the horns, where there is very little variation after the third year of growth.[33] The equation of big horns with sexual success, then, turns out to be another Just So story, one that would not be hard to trace back to long-standing prejudices about masculine aggression, feminine passivity and heterosexual preferences among *humans*.

An ovine reality even harder to explain according to the standard evolutionary theories of sexual selection is that most wild rams, the majority of the time, are homosexual. From the age of five or six years, bighorn males tend to leave their maternal herds and form groups of their own, which Geist cannot help but describe as 'homosexual societies'.[34] Sex occurs throughout the year in these all-male herds, usually in pairs but sometimes in huddles of between three and ten animals, and even when the rams re-join the ewes during the rutting season, a quarter of sexual activity remains homosexual. Some scientific observers, faced with this unavoidable fact, attempt to minimize the sexual nature of the behaviour by calling it 'mounting' and explaining it as 'an expression of dominance' – as George B. Schaller does in his book on Himalayan mountain sheep and goats. (He makes no reference to it in his chapter on 'Courting', confining it instead to a chapter on 'Indirect Aggression'![35]) But this is clearly an inaccurate, or at least a hopelessly partial, explanation. For one thing, so-called 'mounting' between rams, when carried out seriously, involves anal penetration and ejaculation. In such cases, both partners participate, as shown by 'lordosis' in the animal being mounted – that is, the arching of the back in order to facilitate penetration, the same posture adopted by willing ewes during heterosexual mating. Even more tellingly, 'mounting' occurs in the context of a whole range of affectionate behaviours between companionate same-sex pairs: stretching the head and neck low and forward, twisting the muzzle toward the companion while

flicking the tongue and grumbling, kicking a foreleg playfully against the belly or legs, laying the muzzle on the companion's back, or smelling the genitals using the 'flehmen' gesture, where the upper lip is curled back to expose a special olfactory organ. These behaviours account for no less than 70 per cent of inter-actions between rams. Ewes also engage in all of these behaviours with each other, although supposedly with less frequency (unless of course they have simply been observed less frequently, which seems possible given the predilection among ethologists for paying attention to males and the size of their horns).[36]

Since the most salient features of ram anatomy and society – their big horns, their fighting and their sexual activity – seem to be related to their procreative success only tenuously, if at all, how are we to explain them? Perhaps wild sheep confront

Loving body language between bighorn rams.

us, head-on and forcefully, with the need to recognize that not everything in nature can be explained by the Darwinian paradigm of evolution through natural selection. In 1973 Theodosius Dobzhansky wrote an essay combatting American creationists' rejection of Darwinism, which he entitled 'Nothing in Biology Makes Sense Except in the Light of Evolution' – a phrase that has been avidly taken up and repeated often by Darwinian evangelists such as Richard Dawkins.[37] But such a position seems nothing other than a return to fundamentalism – to an absolute faith that a single formula explains the limitless diversity of the organic world.

There are various alternative explanations for the promiscuous clashing and non-reproductive sexual behaviour found among wild sheep. One, of course, is that they do it because it's fun – both fighting and sex are forms of adult play. Another is that they do it out of love – to express and reinforce the bonds of affection among members of their herd. Of course, there's no reason why play, pleasure and love cannot fulfil evolutionary functions – such as assisting the physical and cognitive development of the individual and the cohesion of the herd.[38] It's just that these behaviours in wild sheep are abundantly in excess of what might be required to achieve such goals. For this reason, and because there are so many examples of this kind of profligate expenditure of vital energy in nature, Bruce Bagemihl suggests the term 'biological exuberance' as a way of thinking outside or alongside the Darwinian paradigm. He uses the phrase as the title of a book in which he offers the most compendious available account of non-heterosexual behaviour among animals. Along the way, he shows how, throughout the history of the biological sciences, due to their conventional assumptions about (human) heterosexuality and gender difference, reinforced by a narrow focus on Darwinian sexual selection, ethologists have most often disregarded, or dismissed as anomalous, the great many non-procreative or same-sex sexual behaviours they have observed. By taking these behaviours seriously, Bagemihl seeks to open up a new way of thinking about the diversity of organic life in general. Instead of remaining pre-occupied with 'scarcity (competition for resources) or functionality (the "usefulness" of a particular form of behavior)' as the drivers of biological phenomena, this new model would be based on the perception, following Georges Bataille, that 'all organisms are provided with more energy than they need to stay alive'. This energy, derived ultimately from the sun, is initially spent on growth, but afterwards must be somehow expended (or 'squandered', as Bataille puts it). Accordingly, the prodigally wasteful forms of sexual behaviour among animals, or their more flamboyantly useless adaptations, can be understood as 'mechanisms that "use up" or express this excess energy'.[39] The unnecessarily baroque horns of wild sheep, along with their ground-shaking but in-decisive clashes, and their enthusiastic bouts of non-procreative sex, seem especially good examples of this extravagant dimension of organic life.

While all this is going on among the rams, we might ask, what are the ewes and lambs up to? Again, the traditional biases of human observers have often meant that female sheep are only discussed in relation to reproduction. But of course, as always, there is a lot more to them than that. In fact, it turns out that, in both feral and wild flocks alike, ewes are the central figures.

The fundamental structure of sheep society is the maternal bond between ewe and lamb. This relationship, obviously, is established immediately after birth through maternal care and suckling, but observation of orphaned lambs shows that it is re-inforced and developed subsequently through 'mutual imitation' and 'care and attention'.[40] And it is these initial relationships between lambs and mothers that provide the basis for subse-quent relationships among adult sheep, and thus the organizing structure for the flock in general. Left to themselves, then, sheep are matriarchal: leadership of mixed flocks (when rams are present together with ewes, lambs and juveniles of both sexes), both domestic and wild, belongs to the oldest and most experienced ewe. (Something that ancient writers knew perfectly well: in the first century CE the Roman naturalist Pliny noted that 'it is natural for Rams . . . to follow after old Ewes.'[41]) Sheep society thus challenges our tendency to assume 'that the ability to lead must be demonstrated by some sort of competition or fighting'. On the contrary, 'several different sorts of leadership can exist in the sheep besides that based on fighting, which appeared to have only minor significance'. The elderly ewe who leads the flock is invariably 'inferior in strength and fighting ability to almost any ram, and often inferior to the younger ewes'; her position is achieved 'by the care and feeding of her descendents without, as far as the

A flock of sheep by the water. In self-determining flocks, as here, the eldest ewe provides leadership.

observer can tell, any instance of violence toward her offspring'.[42] This leadership by 'elder stateswomen', confirmed by many other studies, is crucial to normal ovine social organization, since 'the leader of the flock always appears to make decisions about habitat use, and so determine to a large extent the interactions of all others in the group with the environment.'[43] Such a realization perhaps invites us not only to rethink our assumptions about sheep, but indeed about social authority itself; about what it means to lead, to follow, to be an individual, to be part of a society.

It is important to note that these and other fundamental features of sheep social behaviour are seldom observable on commercial farms, partly because

> economic practice demands that ewes be sold when relatively young and that a minimum number of rams be kept, and partly because sheep may be kept either in crowded lots or in such large numbers that leadership cannot be analyzed if indeed it exists at all.[44]

This obvious but easily overlooked point also helps to explain the belief that sheep are exceptionally stupid and passive animals. This assumption has a long and potent cultural history, but it is also reinforced by the way sheep are most often farmed, which prevents the development of the forms of social intelligence fundamental to their natures. Sarah Franklin, one of the most astute and dedicated observers of sheep stereotypes, describes how, on beginning her research on sheep, she wanted to 'learn more about the attribution of stupidity to these animals and frequently asked breeders about this seemingly universal opinion'. Her initial assumption, based on 'over-active ethnographic anticipation', was that 'those who worked with sheep on a daily basis' would have a far more nuanced appreciation of sheep intelligence and more respect for them than is usual. On the contrary, she found herself 'struck by the almost vehement tenacity of the sheep-are-stupid view' among seasoned sheep breeders, who offered her, as 'proof of ovine mental deficiency', endless stories about how sheep are prone 'to particularly "stupid" ways of dying, often by falling head first into places or positions from which they could not extract themselves, or catching their head on obstacles such as fence rails, and then breaking their own necks trying to escape'.[45] It is not hard to imagine how the disruption to natural patterns of bonding, trust and leadership resulting from standard sheep-rearing practices might produce such effects. The great American nature writer Mary Hunter Austin noted this in her account of sheep-rearing in California, *The Flock* (1906):

> Individual sheep have certain qualities, instincts, compe-
> tencies, but in the man-herded flocks these are superseded
> by something which I shall call the flock-mind, though I
> cannot say very well what it is, except that it is less than
> the sum of all their intelligences.[46]

Franklin offers another interesting and persuasive explanation for the durability of beliefs about ovine stupidity. When she raised this question with a Chinese anthropologist colleague, Yunxiang Yan, who had formerly been a shepherd himself, he suggested that the association of sheep with stupidity is

> an artefact of the Western tendency to equate individual-
> ism with intelligence, originality, and leadership. In China
> . . . where conformity is a competitive social skill and the
> point is precisely not to stand out, the sheep is considered
> a highly intelligent animal.[47]

Even so, not all Western farmers have always seen sheep as stupid. The seventeenth-century English farmer and writer Thomas Tryon found his experience as a shepherd sufficient to convince him that sheep possessed not only a language of their own but a rich, emotional inner life. In his *Country-Man's Companion* (1688), Tryon insisted that, by retaining 'that first natural Mother-Tongue, which the Creator endued them with in the beginning', sheep 'can understand by one single bleat . . . the various States, Inclinations and Dispositions of each other, as also express Fullness, Hunger, Love, Hate, Joy, Sorrow, where they should be, and the contrary'.[48]

Another factor to be considered, whenever the question of intelligence among non-human animals arises, is our tendency to value only those kinds of brainpower we take pride in associating with our own species – especially, for example, the kind of rationality that has been central to modern Western ideas of what it means to be human. To this day, scientists prefer to test primates and parrots for linguistic and instrumental intelligence, to see whether they can master (our) semantics and syntax and symbols, to see whether they can solve puzzles, open locks and so on. But these are hardly the most likely or most useful kinds of intelligence to find in a grazing herd animal. All the same, sheep are cleverer even in these particular ways than we usually presume. Merinos tested in mazes, for example, have shown both extensive spatial memories and the capacity to learn from experience.[49] In 2004 newspapers in the United Kingdom were enraptured by the story of sheep in the Yorkshire village of Marsden. These animals, on finding their habitual trot into the village to browse on flowerbeds interrupted by the installation of cattle grids, figured out and then taught their flock-mates how to 'commando roll' across the grids on their backs.[50]

We understand animals far better, though – and humans too – when we accept that there are many forms of intelligence other than this particular brand of tool-manipulating, problem-solving intelligence that modern techno-scientific societies have tended to privilege. Animals, if they are to thrive, need forms of intelligence peculiarly suited to the demands of their habitats and lifestyles. Among herbivorous prey animals who live in herds, the most effective forms of intelligence will be those that emerge out of relationships between the individual and the collective, and will relate to the capacity for assessment of the total environment and the various threats and possibilities it contains. Exceptional evidence of the capacity of sheep in this regard is provided by the phenomenon of 'hefting': the ovine tendency to develop an intense attachment to a particular place. Some breeds are so strongly 'hefted' that they can be farmed without fences. Farmers who use this form of husbandry keep the same flocks in the same area over generations, selecting animals with particularly reliable hefting tendencies for interbreeding.[51] In doing so, of course, they are only manipulating for their own purposes the forms of spatial intelligence typical of all sheep.

One of the particular means by which this intelligence is exercised is described by Geist, based on his observations of bighorns. Sheep who adopt the 'attention posture', which involves freezing and staring in one direction, pricking the ears forward and orienting the body along the line of sight, are signifying that a potential danger has been identified, and the other flock members will immediately look in the same direction and respond accordingly. When an almost-identical (to humans) but slightly less-rigid version of the same posture is adopted, the other sheep easily understand it to mean something quite different – namely, the intention of the posing sheep, often the lead ewe, to move in the direction indicated. Such signals are efficiently relayed among members of the flock, since grazing sheep, although apparently dispersed arbitrarily, actually orient themselves in positions that

enable them to keep an eye on two flock-mates simultaneously – one on each side. (Their horizontal pupils and sideways-facing eyes give sheep panoramic vision of 320 degrees or even more; the human visual field is about 180.)[52]

Sheep coordinate their nearly panoramic vision with one or two flock-mates.

The primatologist Thelma Rowell conducted a study of feral sheep that she specifically designed to challenge the prejudices and assumptions about intelligence and social complexity embodied by comparative psychology's preference for studying animals most like ourselves: that is, other primates. Sheep were chosen as an alternative because they 'are popularly taken as the very paradigm of both gregariousness and silliness', and the study concluded that, at least when they are allowed to flock naturally, sheep display forms of emotional and social

Domestic sheep expressing their love for each other.

intelligence equal to or exceeding those of primates. These include 'an elaborate communicative repertoire and an interactive set of rules for using it'; 'long-term relationships which can carry over periods in which they are not evident'; and techniques for 'assessing and attempting to modify interactions between other sheep', including combinations of behaviours 'akin to reconciliation'. Moreover, 'their ability to lead and to respond to leadership exceeds anything that has been reported for a primate.'[53]

These findings have been dramatically underscored by an experiment that made headlines around the world precisely because it shattered the stereotypes – the byline in *Nature* read: 'the discovery of a remarkable memory shows that sheep are not so stupid after all.' Scientists at the Babraham Institute at the University of Cambridge subjected domestic sheep to a series of tests focusing on facial recognition. They showed their test subjects 25 pairs of photographed sheep faces, some of which were associated with food rewards. The sheep proved able to identify all 50 faces with 80 per cent accuracy, even when shown profiles of faces they had previously only seen head-on, or when the original pairs were broken up. Episodic re-testing showed they could still discriminate between them accurately up to two years later. These findings reflect the fact that sheep share with primates (including humans) a group of cells within the temporal and medial prefrontal cortices of the brain that are specifically designed to encode faces, as distinct from other visual objects, and even to encode preferentially 'the faces of one or more specific familiar individuals'. By recording the responses of these cells to photographs of two individuals previously well known to the test sheep, but from which they had been separated for eight to twelve months, the scientists also showed that sheep remember familiar faces after an absence of at least a year. A non-scientist might think this complex neurological testing unnecessary, since the sheep 'showed clear behavioural signs of recognizing both absent individuals by vocalizing in response to their face pictures'. Beyond the clinical language, we can clearly hear the voices of sheep who are either delighted to see their companions, or distressed at being isolated from them on a Cambridge experimental farm.[54] As Bijal Trivedi put it, writing for *National Geographic News*, the Cambridge study requires us to concede that, 'as they stand huddled with the rest of their flock in what appears like a grazing stupor, sheep may in fact be visualizing long departed flock-mates.' And he cites the lead author of the study, who suggests that 'if sheep have such sophisticated facial recognition skills, they must have much greater social requirements than we thought.'[55]

Thus another default assumption we have about sheep – that they possess no individual identity to speak of – proves to be dead wrong. Just as we make sheepishness idiomatic for stupidity and dullness, we pejoratively describe members of our own species who uncritically go along with the crowd as behaving 'like a flock of sheep'. But as the studies cited above make clear, sheep possess highly acute forms of spatial, social and emotional intelligence, and they are very far from being faceless, insensitive or unthinking towards each other. On the contrary, each flock involves a network of carefully worked-out relationships that take into account both individuals and the collective, and are based on meticulously remembered past experiences.

The Cambridge study found one more thing worth noting here. One of the two previously well-known faces, the ones to which the test sheep responded both neurologically and vocally, belonged

Sheep have a strongly developed capacity to recognize and remember faces – including those of other species.

Sheep displaying the 'attention posture'.

to a sheep, and the other to a human. This demonstrates, of course, that sheep can remember and distinguish between members of our own species no less astutely than they recognize each other.[56] It would seem that, as we look at sheep, they are looking at us – and doing so, most often, more thoughtfully than we are.

3 Ancient Yarns

'It is not too much of an exaggeration to say that the history of man is the history of sheep', writes M. L. Ryder at the start of his encyclopaedic study of human–ovine relationships. Then, a little further on, he qualifies this grandiose claim with the admission that 'in general the sheep appears never to have been important in the history of the Far East.'[1] Perhaps a tendency to overstatement in describing the human–ovine relationship is understandable as compensation for the near-total neglect of the subject among orthodox historians. And no doubt this neglect is explained by the larger tendency to treat sheep as a mass of blank raw material, devoid of interest until transformed into meat, fabric or capital.

If, however, we steer a course between this long-standing neglect of the sheep as a fit subject for history, and the corrective hyperbole of sheep historians, it is reasonable to say that the engagement between *Homo sapiens* and *Ovis aries* has played a fundamental, far-reaching, varied and constitutive role in the history of many aspects of what we call Western civilization, from its first origins to its most recent developments. The formation of the first city-states; the development of writing and accounting systems; the Mesopotamian, Egyptian, Phoenician, Greek and Roman empires; Old Testament Israel; the medieval monasteries; the Vikings; the shift from feudalism to capitalism; the Spanish and British empires; the Industrial Revolution; the emergence of biotechnology – sheep are central to all of these stories.

As mentioned in the previous chapter, the earliest-known account of the sheep occurs in a Sumerian creation myth entitled 'The Debate between Sheep and Grain'. This poem – one of the most ancient written texts extant – begins by describing an early stage in the gods' manufacture of the world, before they had thought up either grain or sheep. 'The people of those days', the poem tells us, 'did not know about wearing clothes; they went about with naked limbs in the land. Like sheep they ate grass with their mouths and drank water from the ditches.' The gods then created sheep and grain on their holy mountain, and sent them down to humankind, where they 'brought wealth to the assembly' and 'sustenance to the land'. The poem goes on to describe how Sheep and Grain, flushed with their success (and with alcohol), debate which of them deserves more prestige. Although the gods ultimately decide that Grain is pre-eminent, the gifts brought by Sheep include clothes, and even 'the gown, the cloth of white wool' worn by the king himself; 'the waterskin of cool water and the sandals' for the workers in the field; 'sweet oil, the fragrance of the gods, mixed oil, pressed oil, aromatic oil, cedar oil for offerings'; and yarn for weapons such as 'the sling, the quiver and the longbows'.[2]

It is noticeable too that this very ancient tale imagines humans themselves, prior to the gift of agriculture, being 'like sheep', grazing and slurping water from ditches. The arrival of domestic animals, along with crops, is necessary to raise people out of an animal existence; *O. aries* is required to transform ovine beings into human beings. The Sumerians, it seems, could not even imagine life before sheep without imagining it in terms of sheep.

The story also bears a similarity to – as well as a marked difference from – the competition between Cain and Abel in the

biblical book of Genesis. These two sons of Adam and Eve, the
first agriculturalists, offer the fruits of their respective labours to
the Lord God. Cain is 'a tiller of the ground' and brings 'fruit
of the ground', while Abel, who is 'a keeper of sheep', makes a
sacrifice of 'the firstlings of his flock and of the fat thereof' (Genesis
1:29; 4:1–16). In contrast to the Sumerian story, Abel's sheep are
judged more valuable by the divinity, and Cain's consequent resent-
ment provokes him to murder his brother. The transition from a
prehistorical existence in the terrestrial paradise – where only
vegetable matter is explicitly identified as food – to the fallen world
of labour, sin and death is marked by agriculture, and specifically
by the high value accorded to the keeping and slaughter of sheep
for human use and consumption.

Both the Sumerian and the Hebrew stories portray the advent
of farming as the cause of new forms of opportunity as well as

new motives for competition, hostility and conflict. No doubt they reflect the real impact of agriculture on the ancient Mesopotamians and Hebrews, and on the other ancient societies that adopted it. The reliable production of food and fibre from crops, sheep and goats would have led to population increases, allowing villages to grow into cities. The production of surpluses would have created communities that could sustain craftspeople specializing in textiles, pottery, tool production and, in due course, metalwork.[3] Meanwhile, population increase and pasture exhaustion would demand the acquisition of new territory, leading to migration but also to invasion and warfare. And so, sheep and sheep-rearing cultures spread over the course of three or four millennia from Mesopotamia to Anatolia, Cyprus, Crete and Greece by about 6000 BCE; and to North Africa a thousand years later. As early as 4000 BCE they had attained their fullest ancient extent, having reached Britain in the west and China in the east.[4] It would be another five and a half millennia before *O. aries* would arrive, at last, in the New World and the Antipodes.

Meanwhile, other developments were both enabled and demanded by the new centrality of crops and flocks. There is little doubt that felt is the most ancient of fabrics: some historians put its origins as far back as 6500 BCE. Felt is made by wetting loose wool fibres and repeatedly pressing them together. Competing legends ascribe the invention of felting to Noah, who observed what happened to the wool that lined the Ark after many days of trampling by his animals, and to St Clement (patron saint of hatters), who put wool in his sandals for added comfort during a long journey, only to find on his arrival that it had transformed miraculously into felt socks.[5]

The implements necessary to spin and weave wool into cloth, however, are also surprisingly ancient. As early as the fourth millennium BCE there were wooden handheld spindles weighted

Earthenware sheep pen from the Chinese Han Dynasty (206 BCE–220 CE). Such objects, placed in a tomb, were supposed to enable the deceased to continue their activities in the underworld.

with whorls, used to spin wool into yarn; looms for weaving yarn into fabric; and dyes for colouring yarn or fabric. The non-moulting fleeces natural to sheep can be plucked by hand or gathered using a comb, but the constantly growing fleece produced by domestication must have been sheared using a single blade until the development of iron technology strong enough to make shears with two blades joined by a spring, which seem not to have appeared until the first millennium BCE.[6]

Sheep-rearing also inspired other new technologies that would, in time, permeate every aspect of human life. Alberto Manguel describes two small clay tablets dating from the third millennium BCE, discovered in 1984 at Tell Brak, Syria: 'simple, unimpressive objects, each bearing a few discreet markings: a small indentation near the top and some sort of stick drawn animal near the centre'; yet as he points out, 'all our history begins with these two modest tablets' because they are 'among the earliest oldest examples of

Clay tablets (most likely) signifying 'ten sheep', from the ancient city of Tell Brak, Syria, late third millennium BCE.

writing we know'. What do they say? 'Observing the delicate incisions portraying animals turned to dust thousands and thousands of years ago, a voice is conjured up, a thought, a message that tells us, "Here were ten goats", "Here were ten sheep."'[7] Both writing and mathematics – or at least, accounting – have their origins in the counting and documenting of flocks. The relationship between sheep-rearing and writing came closer still when sheepskin parchment began to be used for writing with ink, an innovation at least as old as the Egyptian Early Dynastic Period (dating back to the third millennium BCE), and one that lasted in Europe until the importation from China of papermaking techniques during the Middle Ages.[8]

At the same time that sheep-farming was shaping human history, it was also, of course, reshaping sheep. By about 3000 BCE, several millennia of selective breeding had produced sheep smaller in height and horn size than their wild ancestors, with longer tails, whose fleeces – most importantly – were not shed in an annual moult, and were white rather than brown or piebald, and thus better suited to being dyed. Evidence of the emergence of distinct breeds, designed to produce different kinds of wool or meat, begins to appear in the archaeological record in about 2000 BCE, once again in Mesopotamia. Accompanied by the development of related technologies – iron spring-bladed shears for the easier removal of wool, better spindles for spinning it into yarn, richer and more permanent dyes – the new sheep breeds led to the emergence of woollen textile production as a powerful formative influence upon the societies of Mesopotamia, Egypt, the Mediterranean and beyond.[9]

The development of expertise in selective breeding in antiquity is strikingly illustrated by the story of Jacob and Laban in the book of Genesis, which is thought to have been assembled from older sources during the sixth century BCE. In order that he and his family can become independent, Jacob asks his father-in-law Laban, whose flocks he tends, to give him 'all the speckled and spotted cattle, and all the brown cattle among the sheep' – that is, those less valuable animals who would be weeded out in the process of selectively breeding for white fleeces. When Laban agrees, Jacob carries out a breeding programme designed to increase the numbers of speckled and spotted and brown animals. He carves some striped wooden rods and sets them

> in the gutters in the watering troughs when the flocks came to drink, that they should conceive when they came to drink. And the flocks conceived before the rods, and brought forth cattle ringstraked, speckled, and spotted (Genesis 30:25–43).

This account has often been thought to reflect the long-standing belief that a powerful visual impression received by a mother (animal or human) at the moment of conception will be imprinted on her offspring: Jacob's streaked wooden rods thereby produce the same piebald pattern in the lambs. Given the evident practical knowledge of ancient shepherding peoples about how selective breeding works, however, it seems more likely that the story describes Jacob's use of marked fence-posts to enclose the animals he has selected for breeding in order to increase the number of non-white lambs – thereby maximizing the number of sheep he can take from Laban's flock. He knows that, after he has by this means established a large flock for himself, a few generations of subsequent selection will be sufficient to return to white fleeces: white wool, as genetic science would subsequently reveal, is a dominant trait.[10]

The exceptionally high value placed on well-bred wool also lies behind one of the most famous legends of the ancient world:

The exuberantly polycerate Jacob Sheep can have up to six horns, while its piebald fleece means the breed is sometimes apocryphally said to descend from the animals bred by Jacob from the flock of Laban.

the Golden Fleece. Among the many versions of this story, the recurrent theme is the commission of a crew of heroes (in the most familiar version, Jason and his Argonauts) to capture a fleece made of gold from a far-off country, usually identified as Colchis in present-day Georgia on the eastern coast of the Black Sea. To do so, they have to pass through many perils and defeat a dragon, fire-breathing bulls and an army of earth-men grown from serpents' teeth. The Roman historian Strabo, writing in the first century

BCE, suggested that the story's origins lay in the use of especially fine woollen fleeces for collecting gold dust from rivers. Recent historians consider a more likely source to be conflict and competition between ancient societies for possession of fine-woolled sheep breeds, and in particular those capable of producing the pure white fleeces most valuable for dyeing – an interpretation

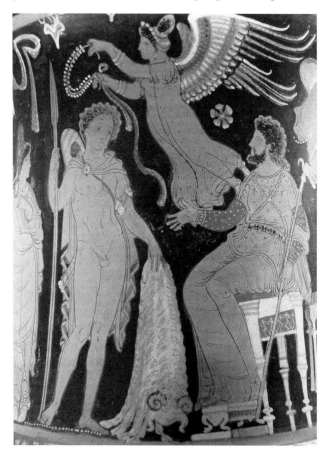

Jason bringing Pelias the Golden Fleece. Decoration on an Apulian red-figure calyx crater, c. 240–330.

reinforced by the fact that in some versions, the fleece is not golden at all, but purple.[11]

There are many other ways in which societies of the ancient world registered the wealth, status and power associated with sheep. The Egyptian supreme god Ammon wore ram's horns as a sign of his pre-eminence, in reference to the more ancient ram-headed god Khnum of Upper Egypt. Khnum, whose name means 'the moulder', embodies the formative importance of sheep: he was said to have fashioned the world and its gods and people on his potter's wheel, using mud from the Nile, and to have power over the development of children in the womb.[12] The Egyptian association of the ram with fertility and potency is impressively registered in the avenue of ram-headed sphinxes leading to the Great Temple at Karnak, while the long-standing association of kingship with pastoral care is embodied by the pharaohs' use of the shepherd's crook as a symbol for their power.

Alongside their place in the iconography of divinity and kingship, sheep leave their mark in the documents and artefacts of the ancient world in ways that show their ubiquity and value

An undated postcard showing the avenue of ram-headed sphinxes leading to the Karnak Temple complex in Egypt.

in everyday life among ordinary folk. In Egypt sheep appear in temple records, on carvings and in sculpture, and were sometimes mummified. Portrayals from the Early Dynastic Period (3000–2000 BCE) show a distinctive corkscrew-horned, lop-eared breed. During the Middle Kingdom (2000–1800 BCE) the more familiar 'Ammon' (curled) horns appear – although sometimes sacred rams and gods were depicted with both kinds of horns. [13]

Sheep played an even greater role in other ancient societies of the Middle East. Vast flocks, numbering between 2,000 and 27,000 animals, are recorded in clay tablets from the third dynasty of Ur (about 2100 BCE).[14] One of the first written codes of law, promulgated by the Babylonian king Hammurabi in about 1772 BCE, includes detailed regulation of the pasturage, shepherding and ownership of sheep, and the harvesting of wool – no wonder, since the famed wealth of his empire was based on wool ('Babylonia' is often said to mean 'Land of Wool').[15] The culture of the ancient Israelites and their patriarchs, too, depended fundamentally on sheep-rearing. According to Ryder, 'there are nearly three hundred references to sheep or lambs in the Old Testament', and most of the major characters are sheep owners. The early books describe the transition of the ancient Israelites from a culture of semi-nomadic pastoralism to one of settled agriculture in Canaan (Palestine). Wool was similarly vital to the economy and culture of the shipbuilding and trading peoples of the ancient Mediterranean: the Phoenicians were famous for their wool dyes, especially their use of murex shellfish to make Tyrian purple, with which they coloured their long woollen cloaks; Carthage exported dyed woollen cloth and carpets; and some of the first coins, said to be minted by the legendarily wealthy Croesus around 550 BCE, were marked with the head of a ram.[16]

Meanwhile, further east, woollen textile was central to the civilizations of the Indus valley, as documented in the *Rig Veda*

Bust of Khnum, c. 305–250 BCE. By this time, the god had acquired both the 'corkscrew' horns of the earliest Egyptian sheep and the curled 'Ammon' horns of the later breeds.

(composed about 1000 BCE). And in the north, the Scythians, who from the eighth to the fourth centuries BCE travelled and plundered from China to the Danube, created their nomadic culture substantially out of wool. They used felt for their tents and for covering the wagons on which they transported their families and possessions. They also wore sheepskins and decorated their tents with coloured pile carpets and woven tapestries.[17]

The philosophers, historians, poets and dramatists of ancient Greece refer many times to sheep-rearing and its products. Indeed, in Greek mythology, human life itself is imagined as a woollen yarn, spun, measured and cut by the three Fates or *Moerae* (*Parcae* to the Romans).[18] The writings of Homer give us perhaps the most 'vivid and natural picture' of the ubiquitous place of sheep in ancient Greece, precisely because, as Ryder points out, the

references are 'incidental to the story being told'.[19] Describing
the Trojans' disorganized response to a Greek assault in the *Iliad*
(composed about 700 BCE), Homer compares them to

> flocks of sheep in a wealthy rancher's steadings,
> thousands crowding to have their white milk drained,
> bleating non-stop when they hear their crying lambs.[20]

His poems show that sheep were integral to the lives of the ancient
Greeks, from the humble shepherds of Ithaca, to the kings and
warriors who make sacrifices of sheep, to the aristocratic women
weaving wool. Book Three of the *Iliad* portrays Helen of Troy herself at the loom,

> weaving a glowing web, a dark red folding robe,
> working into the weft the endless bloody struggles
> stallion-breaking Trojans and Argives armed in bronze
> had suffered all for her at the god of battle's hands.[21]

Relief showing
rams trampling
seed, from the
mastaba of Ti at
Saqqara. Egyptian
Fifth Dynasty,
c. 2430 BCE.

In these extraordinary lines, Homer imagines Helen writing, in woollen thread, the story told by his own lines of poetry: the moment at which the reader reads the story coincides with the moment of its recording by the woman for whose sake it all happens.

A similar intricate link between weaving and storytelling occurs in *The Odyssey*. The protagonist is one of the great tricksters of literature and legend, and two of the best-known ruses in the story rely on the strength and durability of wool. The first is not carried out by Odysseus himself but by his wife. During her husband's ten-year absence, the loyal Penelope keeps her suitors at bay by promising to remarry after she finishes weaving a burial shroud for her father-in-law, but each night she unpicks the work she has completed that day. After years the suitors discover the trick and force her to finish the web, but just as she does so, Odysseus returns home. In this way, Penelope's repeatedly woven and repeatedly teased-apart yarn parallels her husband's digressive, looping, backwards-and-forwards attempts to find his way home.[22]

John William Waterhouse, *Penelope and the Suitors*, 1912, oil on canvas.

Meanwhile, Odysseus survives his most perilous adventure
thanks to the properties of wool, especially its strength and effect-
iveness as a form of concealment. He and his men have been
captured by the Cyclops Polyphemus, who is keeping them
trapped in his cave and devouring them one by one. They have
managed to blind the giant by driving a sharpened olive branch
into his single eye, but they cannot escape because he keeps a
boulder rolled over the mouth of the cave. It is while he is gazing

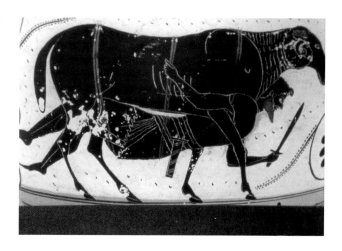

at his captor's beautiful flock of rams, which are also confined in the cave at night, that Odysseus conceives a plan:

> My wits kept weaving, weaving cunning schemes –
> life at stake, monstrous death staring us in the face –
> till this plan struck my mind as best. That flock,
> those well-fed rams with their splendid thick fleece,
> sturdy, handsome beasts sporting their dark weight of wool:
> I lashed them abreast, quietly, twisting the willow-twigs . . .
> three by three; each ram in the middle bore a man
> while the two rams either side would shield him well.

Following the weft of his cunning, Odysseus uses a variation on his more famous trick in the *Iliad*, creating a flock of Trojan sheep to carry his men to safety when the giant lets them out to pasture in the morning. Odysseus himself is forced to cling, at the last moment, to the bellwether:

    tucked up under
his shaggy belly, there I hung, face upward,
both hands locked in his marvellous deep fleece,
clinging for dear life.

Polyphemus, blindly running his hands over the top of each sheep
to ensure the men are not riding out on their backs, notices the
last animal is unusually slow. 'Dear old ram,' he exclaims,

why last of the flock to quite the cave? . . .
Sick at heart for your master's eye
that coward gouged out with his wicked crew?

Here, in the monstrous but pathetic form of the blinded Cyclops
seeking the sympathy of his favourite sheep, we glimpse the kind
of affectionate feeling the ancient shepherd might have felt for
his flock.[23]

Homer's writings bear witness to the pervasive importance
of sheep-rearing throughout ancient Greek society, from the peas-
antry to the aristocracy. And although everywhere in his stories
sheep are killed, eaten or sacrificed, there are other moments
that register their status as living animals, along with a degree of
associated respect – something that will become less common
later in history.

The taken-for-granted importance of sheep was, if anything,
even stronger in Roman culture. According to the mythmakers
and poets of ancient Rome, the city was founded by a shepherd,
Romulus, who with his twin brother Remus had been fostered
by a she-wolf before being adopted into a pastoral family. The
story encodes the very great importance of sheep throughout the
geographical areas and historical period covered by Roman power
and influence. During the second century BCE, the profits of the

Roman republic's successful wars resulted in a reorganization of agriculture along proto-capitalist lines. Although an allotment system distributed small plots to veterans, the wealthy senatorial class invested money gained from foreign conquests into land, amalgamating smallholdings into large-scale estates for the breeding and grazing of sheep, and replacing peasant farmers with slave labour. Wool – and to a lesser extent hides – milk and cheese, were the primary products; sheep were killed for meat relatively infrequently. 'Wool was the major textile fiber of the Roman world', writes Walter O. Moeller: the best-known item in the Roman wardrobe, the toga, was usually made of wool.[24]

The most highly prized of Roman sheep breeds, famous for its very fine fleece, was the Tarentine, which was mainly concentrated in southern Spain; it is sometimes considered the ancestor of the merino. The Romans cosseted sheep as valuable as these. They were stalled in bad weather and hand-fed on barley and split beans, while their fleeces were protected by coats of sacking or hide: hence they were known as *ovis pellitae* (jacketed sheep).[25]

Some of the most important Roman authors devoted their attention to sheep-rearing, in works such as *De agri cultura* (*c.* 160 BCE), written by the famous statesman Cato the Elder during his retirement; the *Georgics* (*c.* 29 BCE) by the great poet Virgil; and *De re rustica* (On Agriculture, *c.* 37 BCE) by the prolific scholar Varro – all of which influenced the most important of all Roman agricultural works, also entitled *De re rustica*, written by Columella in 60 CE. These authors give a very detailed picture of Roman sheep husbandry, including pasturing, breeding, lambing, shearing, milking and the treatment of diseases. Their recognition of the pre-eminent importance of sheep to Rome is best exemplified by Varro, who points out their place in ancient literature:

Of the ancients the most illustrious were all shepherds, as appears in both Greek and Latin literature, and in the ancient poets, who call some men 'rich in flocks,' others 'rich in sheep,' others 'rich in herds'; and they have related that on account of their costliness some sheep actually had fleeces of gold – as at Argos the one which Atreus complains that Thyestes stole from him; or as in the realm of Aeetes in Colchis, the ram in search of whose golden fleece the Argonauts of royal blood are said to have fared forth.

He goes on to argue that the Golden Apples of the Hesperides, gathered by Heracles as one of his twelve heroic labours, were

Hermes Kriophoros (Hermes the Ram-bearer), late Roman.

actually golden sheep, the word *mala* (apples) being an error for *mela*, which the Greeks called sheep 'from the sound of their bleating'. Varro's paean to the 'dignity' of sheep-farming concludes with a simple but (to a Roman) definitive statement: 'Further, does not everyone agree that the Roman people is sprung from shepherds?'[26]

Detailed documentation of agricultural practices becomes far less available during the course of the first millennium CE. As the Roman Empire began to fragment, it was increasingly in the Arab world that knowledge was recorded in a systematic way. But while the great scholars of Islam advanced the disciplines of mathematics, astronomy, biology, medicine, physics and philosophy – in ways that would later be crucial to the European Renaissance – their writings about agriculture were mainly concerned with plant cultivation, and especially irrigation, rather than animal husbandry. Ryder attributes this to the great dichotomy, in Islamic societies of the time, 'between the settled agriculturalist and the nomadic pastoralist, the knowledge of the latter being handed down by word of mouth and never put in writing'. For this reason, he suggests that 'the details of Islamic sheep husbandry must be sought from traditional practices recorded in recent times.'[27]

Many cultures throughout the Middle East, North Africa and Central Asia still depend centrally on sheep-herding. Often, rather than the settled modes of pastoralism discussed so far, these cultures practise various forms of nomadic agriculture. At one end of the spectrum, there is true nomadism, in which whole communities move regularly in search of grazing and water, living in tents assembled and disassembled on the way. At the other end is the practice known as transhumance: the seasonal back-and-forth movement of herds of livestock and their farmers between different regions and climates to allow pasturage throughout the year. So, for example, from ancient times to the present, Kurdish and Bakhtiari sheep-herders of the Zagros Mountains (which extend from modern-day Turkey through Iraq to Iran) have spent their winters on the plains and summers on the high mountain slopes. Comparable journeys have long been undertaken, sometimes twice a year, by the Bedouin of Lebanon, Jordan, Syria and the Arabian Peninsula, the Berbers of North Africa and the various pastoralist peoples of Siberia, Turkestan, Afghanistan, Pakistan, India, Nepal, Tibet and Mongolia.[28]

For many of these cultures, the most valuable product derived from their sheep is milk, along with its processed forms: sour milk, ghee, buttermilk and cheese. But the flock's droppings are also of considerable importance: they are used for fuel. In some areas, wool and woollen goods are highly significant, for example on the Anatolian plateau, where Turkish tribes make the wool into felt used for clothing, rugs and the traditional yurts in which they live. For the most part, these sheep are too valuable to be eaten, although a lamb may sometimes be slaughtered for a special occasion such as a wedding.[29]

In other parts of the Middle East, by contrast, sheep fat is one of the most valuable harvests. The Tartars are said to have dined on rancid mutton fat. Today, as in ancient times, the most distinctive feature of certain breeds favoured by nomadic peoples is the disproportionately fat tail. It seems likely that some populations of wild sheep in arid regions of Mesopotamia evolved longer tails that were bulked up with fat in order to store food; after domestication, selective breeding markedly exaggerated this trait. Fat-tailed sheep have been depicted in art since at least 3000 BCE, and today they are common throughout many parts of Asia and North Africa. The unique type of fat stored in the tail is used in foods, candies and soaps. The tail can comprise 15 per cent of the body weight, and the ram has to push it out of the way with his chest if he is to mate; not all succeed.[30]

In the fifth century BCE Herodotus recorded his admiration for the sheep of Arabia,

> such as are found nowhere else: one kind has such long tails – not less than 4 feet [1.4 m] – that if they were allowed to trail on the ground, they would develop sores from the constant friction; so to obviate this, the shepherds have devised the art of making little carts of wood, and fix one of them under the tail of each sheep.[31]

This remarkable claim has often been repeated over the centuries, for example by Leo Africanus in 1550; by Hiob Ludolf in 1682; by John Dyer in 'The Fleece' (1757), a long Georgic poem in English about shepherding, shearing and the wool trade; and by nineteenth-century experts including William Youatt and Charles Darwin. Other writers – including Rabelais in 1534, Oliver Goldsmith in 1759 and Benjamin Franklin in 1765 – have recounted the story of the fat-tail sheep-trucks ironically, as a way of mocking

Two thousand sheep are driven annually through the streets of Madrid to celebrate Castile's long tradition of transhumance.

contemporary examples of boastfulness and exaggeration.[32] Ryder, despite his magisterial knowledge of all things ovine, seems unsure what to believe: at one point he asserts that 'such two-wheeled carts, harnessed to the animal, have been used for fat-tailed sheep all over the Middle East in recent times', but later he concedes that 'there appears to be no conclusive evidence that [the carts] ever existed'.[33]

There is, of course, no real division between the sheep-farming traditions of these primarily nomadic regions and countries that mostly practise more settled forms of agriculture. Transhumance, at least, was a fundamental mode of sheep-farming in many parts of Europe until a few hundred years ago, and in some areas remains so, although flocks and shepherds now travel by truck (for example from the Mediterranean coast to the French Alps) rather than on foot and hoof.[34] And while the shepherds who actually carry out these migrations may have been peasants for most of history, the management of transhumance by the wealthy and powerful landowners has often been crucial to the way in which pastoralism has impacted on the larger history of nations.

One example will suffice to demonstrate the debt owed by European pastoralism to the nomadic sheep-herders of the Islamic world. In 711 CE the conquest of the Iberian Peninsula by Moors from North Africa brought Arabic and Berber sheep, shepherds and pastoral practices into Spain. That crossing of the narrow strait between continents gave rise to a breed of sheep that would eventually make its way, a thousand years later, to the other side of the world, to Spain's antipodes. But that story, which embodies the crucial role of sheep in the emergence of the modern world, belongs to the next chapter.

4   A Sheep-shaped World

The role played by sheep in the transition from the ancient to the medieval and thence to the modern world is part of a bigger story about human beings' growing power to manipulate organic life on a large scale. A central theme in that story is the relationship between settlement and mobility. From the decline of the Roman Empire to the rise of the British Empire, sheep-farming prospered best – and shaped landscapes and human lives most powerfully – when techniques and breeds that developed in response to specific local conditions were linked into the larger movements and exchanges occurring between countries and across the globe. This is especially clear in the history of Britain and Spain, the two countries that will be the focus of this chapter since they best demonstrate the association between sheep and the emergence of the main forces that shaped the modern world: capitalism, colonialism and industrialization.

The predominance of sheep-farming in Saxon England is suggested by the prevalence of village names employing the prefixes *sceap*, *skip*, *ship*, *shap* and *shep*. This is not surprising given the kinship between Anglo-Saxon culture and that of the Scandinavian Vikings, who were sheep-farmers during winter and voyagers and plunderers in summer. Some of the older British breeds may trace their lineages back to animals introduced by settlers from Scandinavia. The Herdwick breed of the Lake District is sometimes said to have

Herdwick sheep, Lake District, UK.

descended from 40 sheep washed ashore from a Viking vessel wrecked off the Cumberland coast in the tenth century; many consider this story fanciful, but this was a region heavily affected by Norse settlement, and the breed's name suggests a kinship of some kind with Scandinavian breeds: it derives from the Old Norse *herdvyck*, meaning sheep pasture.[1] A similar case can be made for the unique Soay sheep of the St Kilda archipelago off the northwestern coast of Scotland. The most physically 'primitive' breed, in the sense that they bear the closest resemblance to the wild mouflon, Soay sheep are smaller in stature but tougher and more agile than other breeds of *Ovis aries*. Their distinctiveness has been maintained by the isolation of the island of Soay, after which they are named, and which in turn takes its name from them: *Soay* is Old Norse for 'Sheep Island'.[2]

The Norman Conquest of Saxon England was vividly documented in wool – just as Helen of Troy wove the story of the Trojan War. The Bayeux Tapestry, which is not actually a tapestry but a long strip of linen brilliantly embroidered with coloured wool, depicts the whole course of the invasion, including the Battle of Hastings in 1066, in which the Saxons were defeated by William the Conqueror. The subsequent rule by Norman kings and nobles brought changes to English pastoral practices that were to have extremely wide-reaching consequences. In the Domesday Book, a census of England undertaken by the new Norman monarchy in 1086, sheep are more numerous than all other livestock put together. In Saxon England milk had been the main product derived from sheep, but following the Conquest the focus shifted to wool. English wool was highly valued in Europe for its fineness during the twelfth century. As a result, 'the Norman kings soon saw the possibilities of wool exports as a source of revenue, and established a central depot known as the Wool Staple, to collect an export tax on wool.'[3] By the end of the thirteenth century the English barons could make the claim that half their

The death of King Harold, from the Bayeux Tapestry, c. 1070, wool embroidery on cotton.

country's wealth was derived from wool.[4] If this claim was a little
exaggerated, it was nevertheless persuasive. The king whose reign
dominated the following century, Edward III, commanded that his
Lord Chancellor sit on a wool bale while in council, to remind
him of the importance of this commodity to the wealth of the
realm – a tradition continued today in the House of Lords, where
the Lord Speaker sits on the 'woolsack', a cushioned seat stuffed
with wool placed directly in front of the royal throne.[5] Protecting
the wool trade became a decisive element of English foreign policy,
and was a motivating force behind such major events as the Battle
of Crécy in 1346.[6]

The Norman aristocracy possessed large sheep-rearing estates,
but an even more significant role was played by monastic estab-
lishments. Records from wool buyers at the beginning of the
fourteenth century indicate that the monasteries in Yorkshire
alone kept about 250,000 sheep.[7] Of special importance was the
Cistercian order, which arrived from France in 1128 and within
a couple of decades had established 50 monasteries across the
British Isles. The order's very large pastoral estates, highly organized mode of living and proficiency in writing and accounting,

along with the strength of its connections with confrères across the country and continental Europe, allowed it to develop a system of agriculture that anticipated the capitalist economics of future centuries. The Cistercians raised sheep for milk, parchment and wool – the last mostly for export.

A sense of the monastic familiarity with *Ovis* can be discerned, beneath the stylized conventions of the form, in the bestiaries produced by monks in this period. Instead of the single entry

The Speaker's 'woolsack' in the UK House of Lords, directly in front of the steps leading to the throne, *c.* 1880, photograph.

allotted to all other species, the sheep is assigned four – *Agnus* (lamb), *Ovis* (ewe), *Vervex* (wether – that is, castrated ram) and *Aries* (ram) – reflecting the categories within which the meticulous Cistercians inventoried their flocks.[8] And although the bestiarist mostly concentrates on the theological meanings of sheep, he includes some glimpses of the intimate knowledge that comes from close observation. For example, he tells us that the Latin

Lamb (*Agnus*) and wether (*Vervex*) from an English bestiary, late twelfth century.

Lambs seeking out their mothers in a scene from a 13th-century English bestiary.

word for lamb, *agnus*, derives from *agnoscere*, to recognize, 'because above all other animals it is able to recognise its mother', knowing her bleat even 'in the middle of a large flock' and running to her, just as she in turn 'will pick out her lamb among many thousands of others' even though 'their bleating appears to be the same, and they all look alike'.[9] This idea first appeared in the *Etymologies* of Isidore of Seville, but the bestiarist does not attach a religious meaning to it in the usual way; rather, its inclusion and its vividness surely derive from first-hand knowledge of the lamb–ewe relationship, which is primary to flock behaviour.

The Cistercians enjoyed significant advantages over non-monastic pastoralists. As members of the clerical domain they were exempt from taxes levied by the Crown, and they were also able to open up markets and negotiate prices throughout Christendom by means of their strong international connections. Their trade networks operated not just through the other Cistercian monasteries in Europe but through a fraternal order specifically tasked with travel: the Knights Templar. This order of fighting monks was approved by Pope Honorius II in 1129, following the first Crusade, on the advice of Bernard of Clairvaux, who was the Cistercians' own founder and who used their rules as the basis for those of the new order. The Templars farmed on the Cistercian model, but they also acquired many ships, with which they transported troops and pilgrims to the Holy Land, along with cargoes of wool from their Cistercian brothers.[10]

Such was the web of influence spun by wool traders, religious and lay, that during the medieval period, as Robert Trow-Smith writes, 'the quality, price and quantity of British wool could bring prosperity or ruin to the weavers of Flanders, the flock-masters of Spain, the merchants of Italy.' He suggests that this 'change from an individual, self-subsistent stock husbandry, such as had been practised in Britain for nearly 4,000 years, to a vast network of industry and commerce founded upon a humble sheep on this same common was as immense as any in history'.[11]

Other features of the Cistercian agricultural enterprise also helped establish the groundwork for the later emergence of capitalism. These included a form of vertical integration whereby their various estates were subdivided into granges that specialized in different activities, and the granges into different stages in the process of wool production: maintenance and feeding of flocks, washing and shearing, transport and sale of wool and so on. Another was the Cistercians' early adoption of technological innovations that anticipated industrialization: they built elaborate sewage systems, made use of water power and even seem to have pioneered a primitive kind of blast furnace for smelting iron, using the phosphate-rich slag as fertilizer.[12]

Perhaps the most influential aspect of Cistercian sheep-farming, however, was the way they abandoned the system of dividing land into small strips – as practised on the estates owned by the feudal aristocracy, which were farmed by peasant tenants

– and instead opened up huge pastures for running flocks that numbered in the thousands. This system radically reduced the amount of human labour required to farm large flocks, and took over previously unusable land through the agency of the sheep themselves, whose manure and grazing created rich pasture out of 'wasteland'. And it was this model of agriculture that would produce the most rapid and radical change in the English social order when it was adopted by English feudal landowners. During the sixteenth century they too began enthusiastically 'enclosing' land; that is, converting small tenanted allotments, many of them previously planted in crops, into vast areas of pasturage for sheep. In the process, they drove off the peasant farmers who had worked and lived in those locations for generations. The resulting social upheaval and shift in economic structure was a pivotal point in the transition of feudalism into capitalism. The effects included the creation of a large unemployed class and rapidly rising commodity prices – phenomena rare in a feudal system but endemic to capitalism.[13]

These enclosures and their social consequences were vividly decried in 1516 by Thomas More in his satire *Utopia*, within which a diatribe by the Portuguese traveller Raphael Hythloday begins with a sensational claim. 'Your sheep,' he tells the Lord Chancellor of England,

Bellwether and flock of sheep, c. 1300, English bestiary.

that are commonly so meek and eat so little; now, as I hear, they have become so greedy and fierce that they devour human beings themselves. They devastate and depopulate fields, houses and towns.

Having captured his audience's attention with this startling claim, he explains what he means by it:

For in whatever parts of the land sheep yield the finest and thus the most expensive wool, there the nobility and gentry, yes, and even a good many abbots – holy men – are not content with the old rents that the land yielded to their pre-decessors . . . they leave no land free for the plough: they enclose every acre for pasture; they destroy houses and abolish towns, keeping the churches – but only for sheep-barns. Thus, so that one greedy, insatiable glutton . . . may enclose thousands of acres within a single fence, the tenants are ejected . . . They would be glad to work, but can find no one who will hire them. There is no need for farm labour . . . One herdsman or shepherd can look after a flock of beasts large enough to stock an area of land that used to require many hands to make it grow crops.

As well as creating a large new class of unemployed, he goes on to point out that 'this enclosing has led to sharply rising food prices in many districts', while 'the price of raw wool has risen so much that poor people among you who used to make cloth can no longer afford it', because the wool trade 'is concentrated in so few hands . . . and these so rich, that the owners are never pressed to sell until they have a mind to, and that is only when they can get their price'.[14] It would be hard to find, prior to Marx and Engels, a clearer critique of capitalism.

The pace of enclosure, however, was only to accelerate during the reign of Henry VIII. Motivated partly by anticlericalism, partly by determination to divorce his first wife against the will of the Roman Catholic Church and partly by the desire to transfer wealth from church to state, Henry (through the zealous agency of his chief minister, Thomas Cromwell) dissolved the English monasteries and seized their assets between 1536 and 1541.[15] The scale and intensity of these developments were such that Karl Marx identified them as crucial precursors to the eventual emergence of industrial capitalism:

> Land grabbing on a great scale, such as was perpetrated in England, is the first step in creating a field for the establishment of agriculture on a great scale, [because it] concentrates the instruments of labour in the hands of a few . . . The labourers are first driven from the land, and then come the sheep.[16]

Elsewhere Marx identifies wool produced in the British Isles during the sixteenth century with the initial appearance of capital, insofar as it 'offers at the early stages a constant excess of market-price over price of production during the rise of industry'.[17] In these various ways, as Salisbury puts it, 'the wool of the sheep defined the transition to commercial life that marks the modern world'.[18]

So it is that, in Shakespeare's *The Merchant of Venice* (1597), Shylock the moneylender tells the story of Jacob's breeding of 'parti-coloured lambs' from Laban's flock: 'and those were Jacob's. / This was a way to thrive'. Antonio assumes the story is being told as a justification for usury: 'Was this inserted to make interest good?' he asks, 'Or is your gold and silver ewes and rams?' Shylock responds to this scorn with quick wit: 'I cannot tell, I make it breed as fast' (Act I Scene III). In this exchange, Shakespeare demonstrates the early modern suspicion – here, as so often, projected hypocritically onto the stereotype of the Jew – of the emerging capitalist practice of investment lending, while at the same time demonstrating the easily recognizable association of capital with sheep.

Meanwhile, Spain was becoming Britain's main competitor in wool production. This was due to the emergence of the merino, which by the seventeenth century was recognized as the best sheep in the world for producing fine wool. The origins of the breed probably involved the interbreeding of the fine-woolled Tarentine breed of Roman Spain with North African animals introduced by the Moors. According to the *Oxford English Dictionary*, the name *merino* most likely derives from the Arabic '*Marīnī*, member of the Banū Marīn, a Berber people and former dynasty of Morocco . . . from whose territory sheep were imported to Spain.' When the system used today for assessing wool fineness is applied to samples from that time, Spanish wool is as fine as 21 microns (a micron is one thousandth of a millimetre), whereas the finest

Illustration of Don Pedro, one of the first merino rams in the USA, who arrived on a Delaware farm owned by the du Pont family from France in 1801. When Don Pedro died, the du Ponts received condolences from Thomas Jefferson.

DON PEDRO

Elisabeth Frink's Shepherd and Sheep sculpture (1975) in London's Paternoster Square commemorates the site's historical role as a livestock market.

British wool available is 26 – and that is from the Ryeland breed, which was never as plentiful as the merino.[19]

Spanish merinos were managed by transhumance, driven in herds as large as 10,000 animals between summer and winter pastures. As Eileen Power points out, such vast flocks feature in Miguel de Cervantes's *Don Quixote de la Mancha* (1605), in which the would-be knight and his squire encounter transhumant merinos 'on their great annual trek from their summer pastures in the north uplands to the winter pastures in the plains of Estremadura and Andalusia'.[20] Don Quixote and his squire Sancho Panza are trotting along, discussing chivalry, when they see two great palls of dust approaching. In fact, these clouds are 'raised by two flocks of sheep which chanced to be driven from different

parts into the same road, and were so much involved in the cloud of their own making, that it was impossible to discern them until they were very near'. To Don Quixote, however, whose 'imagination was engrossed by those battles, enchantments, dreadful accidents, extravagant amours and rhodomontades, which are recorded in books of chivalry', the dust clouds are produced by 'two armies in full march to attack each other', and the situation offers a perfect opportunity to fulfil his knightly duty 'to assist and support that side which is weak and discomfited'. He has no trouble identifying one side as belonging to 'the mighty emperor Alifanfaron, sovereign of the great island of Taproban', and the other to 'his mortal enemy king of the Garamanteans' – that is, a Muslim and a Christian ruler respectively. Watching the convergence of the flocks from a hilltop, Don Quixote describes to Sancho the various knights, along with their 'arms, colours, mottos and devices', whom he perceives doing battle in the dust storm beneath. When Sancho confesses he cannot hear 'the neighing of steeds, the sound of clarions, the noise of drums', but only 'the bleating of ewes and lambs', his master concludes with pity that his squire's fear has disordered his senses. When Don Quixote judges the time right for action, he rides 'into the thickest of the squadron of sheep' and begins 'to lay about him, with as much eagerness and fury, as if he had been actually engaged with his mortal enemy'. The shepherds eventually manage to knock him from his horse with their slingshots and, 'gather[ing] together their flock with all imaginable dispatch, and taking their dead, which might be about seven in number, upon their shoulders', they leave him unconscious on the road. When Sancho rejoins him, Don Quixote dejectedly admits that his imaginary enemy Freston the magician, 'envying the glory I should have gained in this battle, hath doubtless metamorphosed the squadrons of the foe into flocks of sheep'.[21]

Don Quixote's ovine delusion. Illustration by Chris Riddell to *Don Quixote* (retold by Martin Jenkins, London, 2009 edition).

For all Don Quixote's craziness, his encounter reflects the awe felt by many who recorded the huge regiments of sheep that crossed and re-crossed the peninsula – during which 'the sheep were said to keep admirable order'[22] – as well as the power and wealth represented by these movements. The Spanish transhumances were controlled by a national association, the Mesta, created in the thirteenth century. Such was the economic importance of merino wool that this organization came 'to dominate the whole of Spanish economy and subordinate agriculture entirely to its demands'.[23]

Recognition of the pre-eminent fineness of merino wool created a growing competition between Spain and Britain for domination of the European trade. Export of merinos was made a capital offence in Spain, although in the eighteenth century the Spanish Crown eventually itself made gifts of merino sheep to Sweden, Germany and France, leading to further diversification of the breed. At the end of that century Joseph Banks, who became famous as the naturalist on James Cook's Pacific voyage of 1769 and was now President of the Royal Society, advocated for the importation of merinos into Britain, and brought some from Spain to George III's experimental farm at Kew Gardens. The merino never became well established in Britain, but Banks's efforts paid off in a different direction, since the breed was to form the basis for the immense flocks established during the ensuing century in Britain's colonies Australia and New Zealand.[24]

Sheep had long been part of the process that Alfred Crosby calls 'ecological imperialism', whereby Europeans introduced their domestic animals to the territories they colonized. Not only did this provide the colony with a readymade agricultural economy, it altered the host terrain, sculpting it into an ecological shape that fitted the designs of the settlers: 'because these animals are self-replicators,' writes Crosby, 'the efficiency and speed with which they can alter environments, even continental environments, are superior to those of any machine we have thus far devised.'[25]

Christopher Columbus – who came from a Genoese family of wool-weavers – introduced sheep and other domestic animals to the Americas on his second voyage in 1493, and these were augmented by Hernán Cortés when he invaded Mexico in 1519. These first ovine immigrants were probably churros, a hairy Spanish breed, but merinos were also introduced in 1540.[26] And as Elinor Melville describes, while the conquistadors were violently invading, their sheep were quietly changing the terrain in ways inimical to native peoples and species alike. Old World animals brought with them pathogens to which indigenous humans and animals were immunologically defenceless; they also altered the landscapes by 'radically changing the vegetative cover'. At the same time, gently but relentlessly, they despoiled the crops and gardens of the native peoples, since they were allowed to wander indiscriminately. In Mexico 'the Spanish pastoralists treated the Central Highlands as an open commons, as they had in Spain', allowing 'uncontrolled grazing by vast armies of sheep'. So it was that, as early as the mid-1560s, 'sheep gained the ascendency both in the lands they utilized and in their numbers.'[27] By the start of the twentieth century, proponents of wilderness conservation such as John Muir – demonstrating the ease with which humans make other species into the scapegoats for their own environmental sins – were describing sheep in the American Southwest as 'hoofed locusts'.[28]

By the end of the eighteenth century, the British, too, had mastered the use of pastoralism as a means to dispossess inconvenient populations. In the aftermath of their defeat at the Battle of Culloden in 1745, Highland Scots found themselves systematically displaced by their own lairds through the process of enclosure, driven by the growing demand for wool and meat in England. In one case, 'four shepherds, their dogs and three thousand sheep now occupied land that had once supported four townships.'[29] The breed used in this context was the Cheviot, a recently developed and exceptionally hardy animal, virtually purpose-bred to thrive in the harsh Scottish climate. The process of enclosure came to a climax in 1792, subsequently called 'the Year of the Sheep', when riots and uprisings led to the forced exile of many Highlanders and the forced clearances of the following decades. This process 'set an important precedent for the colonization of Britain's overseas possessions, in particular Australia, where an invasion of white settlers was facilitated by a swelling tide of white sheep'.[30]

Coigach in the Scottish Highlands, a region subject to the Clearances well into the 19th century.

White Australians regard their settlement of the great southern continent as beginning with the arrival of the first fleet in Botany Bay and Port Jackson (which would become Sydney) in January

1788. These eleven ships carried several hundred convicts, along with guards and officers and their families, to supply labour and inmates for a British penal colony. The ships also carried about 90 sheep, but these were intended for consumption rather than farming, and few survived beyond the first year of the settlement.[31] However, the British government intended the colony to become economically self-sufficient as soon as possible, and to this end, more shipments of sheep were sent over the next few decades. The result was the rapid establishment of a thriving pastoral economy. In addition, as they had in the Americas, sheep were deployed as agents for the expansion of white settlement, the corresponding displacement of indigenous Australians and the transformation of the endemic ecosystem. 'Indeed the settlement of New South Wales, often referred to as Australia's first frontier, was largely a settlement by sheep.'[32] The state had 9 million sheep by 1845 and 12 million a decade later. The settlers claimed land easily through the acquisition of squatter's licences; half the continent had been settled this way by 1840. Expansion was largely driven by exhaustion of the land, which could happen within a decade or less. Overgrazing and trampling by millions of hard hooves – which the Australian ecosystem had not encountered before – swiftly killed off ground cover and compacted the soils, resulting in less rain and a reduced ability to absorb moisture, along with increased instability and liability to erosion on slopes. The geologist and botanist Paul Edmund de Strzelecki vividly described the results in a survey from 1841:

> Dews began to be scarce, and rain still more so: one year of drought followed another; and in the summer of 1838, the whole country of New South Wales . . . presented with very few exceptions a naked surface without any perceptible pasture upon it for the numerous half-starved flocks.[33]

As native plants and animals were devastated, the native Australians who depended on them had no choice but to abandon their lands, or to participate in pastoralism, either through sheep-rustling or working for those white settlers willing to have them. Just as in the Americas, then, an agricultural invasion accompanied the more overt and brutal violence carried out by white settlers against the aboriginal population.

Observers like Strzelecki showed that the destructive aspects of the pastoralists' triumphal march were visible at the time, but ignored because the economy was thriving. The period of the wool boom between 1822 and 1851 has become known to historians as Australia's 'Great Pastoral Age'. James Collier, writing in 1911, gave the story in epic terms, drawing on the ancient history of pastoralism – comparing the settlers to 'the patriarchs of old', referring to the whole of Australian society and culture as 'the work of the Golden Fleece' – in order to present Australian agri-colonialism as part of the great onward advance of civilization.[34] That Collier's narrative reflected a widespread perception is demonstrated by the common claim, repeated well into the twentieth century, that Australia was 'riding on the sheep's back'.[35]

The origins of Australian pastoralism are closely tied up with the name of Captain John Macarthur, who arrived in Sydney in 1790 as a prison superintendent. He established sheep on the land at Parramatta he was granted as an officer, which he called Elizabeth Farm. By the end of the century he had acquired merinos from South Africa, and set about establishing his claim to breed the purest merinos in the new colony – acquiring more stock from the British Royal flock, regardless of bitter quarrels with Sir Joseph Banks and others. Despite, or perhaps thanks to, his rebarbative temperament, Macarthur eventually succeeded in creating – or at least he claimed credit for creating – an Australian stock of merinos of sufficient size and quality that, by the time of his death in 1834, British imports of wool from Australia were greater than those from Spain. As Franklin points out, Macarthur's contribution to this outcome is open to dispute: for one thing, 'opinion remains divided as to whether Macarthur's sheep were particularly significant to the emergence of the fine-wool industry in Australia'; for another, it was actually Macarthur's wife Elizabeth who managed the livestock on the estate named after her during the lengthy periods in which her husband was 'spinning' his sheep in London. And, of course, there were other dedicated breeders who played crucial roles. The Reverend Samuel Marsden of Parramatta, for example, established a more cooperative relationship with Joseph Banks and did a much better job than Macarthur of pleasing his patrons: when he visited Britain in 1807 he had a suit made of his own merino wool, which he wore to an audience with George III, who was so impressed he asked for a coat made from the same material, in return for which he gave Marsden five pregnant merino ewes. Nevertheless, it is Macarthur's role in the establishment of one of Australia's historically most significant industries that was commemorated on the country's $2 note, which for many years featured his portrait alongside that of a merino ram.[36]

For the merino the next step was all but inevitable – the step that would complete the breed's long journey from Spain to that country's exact antipodes. In the middle of the nineteenth century, as the British demand for fine wool continued to grow, colonial pastoralism sought fresh fields and pastures in New Zealand – a country that, with its wetter temperate climate, seemed an immediately more rewarding prospect than Australia. During the 1830s and '40s, Australian merinos were taken to New Zealand in large numbers, but soon breeding within the country took over. During the 1850s and '60s, the ready availability of free land, free grass and a large local market could mean staggering profits for those first in. 'Sheep farming', observed the *Otago Witness* in the 1850s, 'presents visions of quite dazzling wealth'.[37]

There were over a million sheep in the country by 1860, 13 million by 1880 and 20 million by the end of the century.[38] For considerably more than a century, sheep farming provided the most effective lure for new settlers, the longest-enduring major source of economic growth, and the strongest driver of environmental transformation in Britain's last and furthest-flung colony.

Emigration to New Zealand, unlike emigration to Australia, was driven largely by organized private enterprise. The colonial entrepreneur Edward Gibbon Wakefield used his New Zealand Company agents to promote settlement to prospective emigrants. In so doing, they drew on the fertile landscapes and idealized social relations of the European pastoral and Arcadian traditions, creating New Zealand as an agricultural utopia in the mind's eye of the intending emigrant.

An Australian $2 note, discontinued in 1988, featuring a merino ram and John Macarthur, one of Australia's founders and pioneer of the Australian wool industry.

Originating in antiquity – going back to the shepherds of Homer and the *Eclogues* and *Georgics* of Virgil – the pastoral and Arcadian genres had gained a new life in British art and literature from the Renaissance onwards. Both forms portray rural life as a world of natural simplicity and authenticity, usually in contrast to the over-refinement and corruptions of city life. In the pastoral, which contrasts the hardships and harvests of seasonal and meteorological change, the central figure of the shepherd with his flock embodies a healthy pattern for the travails of life. In Edmund Spenser's *Shepheard's Calendar* (1579), for instance, each month's poem focuses on the shepherds' musings on love, age and faith, which are embodied by the sufferings and flourishings of their sheep. So in March two young shepherds rejoice that the 'grasse now ginns to be refresht' and tell each other stories about Cupid, while in February the flock is

Tom Roberts, *Shearing the Rams*, 1890, oil on canvas.

'clothed with cold, and hoary with frost', the rams without 'corage', the ewes with 'blowen bags', the early lambs 'starved with cold', because the shepherd 'their Maister is lustelesse and cold'.

The related Arcadian genre was less true-to-life, more idealizing; it tended to portray a faux-classical world of amorous shepherds and shepherdesses, set amid a fertile landscape of fruiting trees and gentle livestock. Thus, for example, the emphatically urban Christopher Marlowe, in his poem 'The Passionate Shepherd to his Love' (1599), epitomizes the Arcadian fantasy:

> Come live with me and be my love,
> And we will all the pleasures prove . . .
>
> There will we sit upon the rocks,
> And see the shepherds feed their flocks . . .
> A gown made of the finest wool
> Which from our pretty lambs we pull;

Edward Calvert, *The Sheep of His Pasture*, 1828, line engraving on paper.

The shepherd swains shall dance and sing
For thy delight each May-morning . . .

From the eighteenth century onwards pastoral and Arcadian art and literature provided a kind of imaginary compensation for a population that was increasingly urbanized and thereby separated from rural life. The enduring power and appeal that these traditions held for the Victorians can be seen in Thomas Hardy's popular novel *Far from the Madding Crowd*, first published in serial form in the *Cornhill Magazine* in 1874. The plot concerns the intertwined romantic and working lives of Gabriel Oak, a shepherd; Bathsheba Everdene, who inherits a farm and decides to run it with Oak's help; and William Boldwood, a prosperous neighbouring farmer. The characters' emotional vicissitudes occur in the midst of vividly evoked pastoral routines and crises: new lambs brought inside to be hand-reared by the fire, sheep-washing and shearing, a flock driven over a cliff by an inexperienced dog, animals afflicted by bloat from gorging on clover, a village sheep fair. Throughout it all the authenticity of the pastoral estate is embodied by Gabriel Oak, a character as solidly rooted in nature as his surname, who plays the flute 'with Arcadian sweetness'. An extended description of shearing allows Hardy to draw the clearest contrast between the values of the transient modern world of Victorian progress and the abiding traditional world of the pastoral estate. We are told that the medieval barn where the shearers bring the sheep 'embodied practices that had suffered no mutilation at the hands of time . . . So the barn was natural to the shearers, and the shearers were in harmony with the barn.' It is this sense of connection between nature, worker and life that, by the end of the novel, brings together in marriage our two favourite characters, Gabriel and Bathsheba, who are joined not 'in their pleasures merely' but 'in their labours'.[39]

The novel appeals as a nostalgic evocation of a world slipping away in Victorian Britain. But proponents of emigration to the colonies found it possible to represent this kind of updated Arcadia as a real and viable future, accessible to those willing to make the voyage to the other side of the globe. So it is that Herbert Guthrie-Smith (with the irony of hindsight) recalls how he felt as a young settler, newly arrived from Scotland, breaking in his farm in 1878:

Thomas Cole, *The Arcadian or Pastoral State*, 1834, oil on canvas. This painting, the second in Cole's series *The Course of Empire*, shows his Romantic notion of the ideal relationship between human society and nature.

For a young man what an ideal existence! – to make a fortune by the delightful labour of your hands – to drain your swamps, to cut tracks over your hills, to fence, to split, to build, to sow seed, to watch your flock increase – to note a countryside change under your hands from a wilderness, to read its history in your merinos' eyes. How pastoral! How Arcadian![40]

And Samuel Butler, who as a young man spent four years establishing a sheep station in New Zealand, opens his famous satirical novel *Erewhon* with the naive Arcadian vision of the new settler:

> The harbours were sufficient; the country was timbered, but not too heavily; it was admirably suited for agriculture; it also contained millions on millions of acres of the most beautifully grassed country in the world, and of the best suited for all manner of sheep and cattle. The climate was temperate, and very healthy; there were no wild animals, nor were the natives dangerous, being few in number and of an intelligent tractable disposition.[41]

William Holman Hunt, *Our English Coasts* (also called *Strayed Sheep*), 1852, oil on canvas.

Of course this description, based on Butler's own experience of the New Zealand province of Canterbury in the 1860s, ignores the strenuous labour by which human beings had constructed this idyll: the cutting or burning of the native forest, the draining of the wetlands that originally covered the plains and the introduction of European grasses.

It also emphatically misrepresents (to serve Butler's deliberate satirical ends, as it turns out) the real relationship between the colonial government and the indigenous Māori population, who were at the time engaged in a series of long and bitter wars. The Treaty of Waitangi had been signed in 1840 between representatives of the British Crown and a number of local *rangitira* (chiefs), but in the ensuing decades the colonial government increasingly acquired Māori land by illicit means, provoking a series of protracted land wars. Far from being harmless, few and tractable, like the 'natives' referred to by Butler's narrator, Māori proved to be well armed, well organized and more than capable of adapting their vigorous warrior traditions to the modern world. Despite the inexorable tide of Crown troops, they won many victories and staved off defeat for longer than expected, coming up with new tactics ranging from trench warfare to passive resistance. But the disproportionate weight of the British Empire made the eventual outcome inevitable, and region by region, those who continued to resist had their land confiscated by the Crown, and their *pā* (fortified villages) and crops replaced by flocks of imported sheep nibbling imported grasses.[42]

The definitive influence of pastoralism in New Zealand's modern destiny was further strengthened in 1882 when the ship *Dunedin* set sail for Britain with the first shipload of frozen mutton and lamb. Refrigerated shipping allowed the vast expansion of meat and wool production for export to the British market, which fundamentally shaped the social, political and economic

Sheep in lairage at Freezing Works, Belfast, New Zealand, 1960s.

character of New Zealand for the next century.[43] Throughout that time, pastoralism continued to expand: 100 years after the inauguration of refrigerated shipping, the country's sheep population peaked at 70 million.[44] It is almost entirely to the traffic in ovine fleece and flesh that we owe the stereotypical New Zealand landscape of the twentieth century: plains or rolling paddocks dotted with sheep all the way to a horizon marked by snowy mountains. From a land of forests and wetlands, New Zealand in the nineteenth and twentieth centuries was transformed into a land of pasture, a kind of off-site, nation-sized farm for the British Empire.

The process, or rather its meticulous observation and vivacious documentation, has yielded a classic of New Zealand literature – indeed, of nature writing in general. Herbert Guthrie-Smith's *Tutira: A New Zealand Sheep Station*, first published in 1921 – although Guthrie-Smith continued to add to it until his death in 1940 – is the ecological biography of the author's Hawke's Bay sheep run. His intimate and precise documentation of the interaction between his sheep and his land provides an unusually thoughtful account of the ways in which *Ovis aries* has shaped countries like New Zealand. So, for example, the title of the chapter that describes the initial surveying and landscaping of Tutira, 'The Chartographers of the Station', refers not to *Homo sapiens* but to *Ovis aries*. 'It is sheep that have surveyed Tutira', writes Guthrie-Smith: 'the first action of a mob in a strange enclosure [is] to map it out, to explore it, that is, by lines radiating from established camps.' In this way, over time, the best tracks and crossings are discovered, while treacherous localities, those 'mined with underrunners, blind oozy creeks, cliffs and so forth are avoided'.[45] The sheep-paths thereby laid down, in time, allow the shepherds to access the run, and eventually are incorporated into human traffic networks.

Guthrie-Smith thus notices and records, with remarkable precision, the process of environmental change that colonial agriculture brings about. As a young and struggling farmer trying to 'break in' a recalcitrant piece of land, he feels admiration and gratitude – at least initially – for the path-breaking labour of his sheep: hence his delight in describing instances of sheep 'architecture'. Not only do the hooves of his flocks cut tracks into the ground, he tells us, they also build 'viaducts'. They do so simply by the habitual action of walking along the curved ridges that run between hilltops as they pass to and from their feeding grounds. They prefer these routes because they are merinos, members of 'an easily scared breed' who feel safer 'on the heights'. As a result, they gradually build up causeways at the lowest points of the ridges,

> as if the little builders were deliberately taking thought of the morrow, scheming to save themselves toil. The tools of the sheep are his toes, his sharp hoofs act as gouges and chisels in the work; rain, sun, and wind, carrying down silt and dust from the heights on either side, supply building material; the centre of the path constantly scooped out is as constantly refilled.

Fascinated, Guthrie-Smith watches these viaducts 'increase, inch by inch, until after forty years their height has risen to a yard and a yard and a half. The finished article, its close-nibbled verdant banks fed with rich dust and silt, is a beautiful bit of animal architecture.' Other ovine public works include 'returfing the naked windblows, hardening the erst-while dangerous fords, drying the bogs and marshes . . . exposing pitfalls and chasms'.[46]

Guthrie-Smith does not confine himself merely to documentation of the changes brought about by his sheep: he also registers

Angela Singer,
Ghost Sheep, 2001,
240 preserved
sheep skins
discarded by
a skin processing
plant.

his growing unease with the process. His successive revisions of the manuscript demonstrate increasing alarm at the impact of his farming practices on the local environment. By the end of his life he has come to a position that radically questions the entire project of pastoralism. In 1940, the year of his death, when he published the third edition of *Tutira*, he lamented that 'the country under my régime has been shorn of its fleece', and warns that 'in the time to come it will be flayed of its very skin.' Looking back with typical honesty on his life's work, he concludes that the ultimate aim of observing the myriad agencies at work on his land has been to understand better and respect better 'the rights of the land', to recognize 'in it something more than the ability to grow meat and wool'.[47] In the preface to this edition, he wonders frankly whether he has 'for sixty years desecrated God's earth and dubbed it improvement'.[48] In this way Guthrie-Smith challenges head-on the ideology fundamental to the interlinked projects of eighteenth- and nineteenth-century modernity – namely, the commitment to the large-scale reorganization of territories, peoples, environments and species as dictated by the idea of industrial, capitalist and imperialist 'progress'.

5 Little Lamb, Who Made Thee?

One cold September day in the 1720s, a man descended the Pennine Hills, leaving the snow behind, and entered the valleys of Yorkshire's West Riding district. He described the scene that opened out before him:

> we found the country one continued village . . . hardly an house standing out of a speaking-distance from another; and as the day cleared up, we could see at every house a tenter, and on almost every tenter a piece of cloth, kersey, or shalloon; which are the three articles of this country's labour. [A traveller is agreeably struck with the diversified scene that these parti-coloured cloths exhibit.] In the course of our road among the houses, we found at every one of them a little rill or gutter of running water . . . and at every considerable house was a manufactory.[1]

This is Daniel Defoe, describing his journey through the heart of the British wool-producing district in his *Tour through the Whole Island of Great Britain* (1727). 'Kersey' is a kind of coarse woollen cloth; 'shalloon' is a lightweight woollen fabric, used, for example, in coat linings; a 'tenter' is the frame upon which these cloths are hung – hence the expression 'on tenterhooks' – to dry out after 'scouring' (which washes away dirt, grease and lanolin from the raw wool) and dyeing. To Defoe, with his businessman's eye, the valleys of the West Riding are a kind of manufacturing utopia:

> Though we met few people without doors, yet within we saw the houses full of lusty fellows, some at the dye-vat, some at the loom, others dressing the cloths; the women and children carding, or spinning; all employed from the youngest to the oldest; scarce any thing above four years old, but its hands were sufficient for its own support. Not a beggar to be seen, nor an idle person.[2]

We might suspect Defoe of idealizing what he sees: 'the people in general live long', he continues, because 'under such circumstances hard labour is naturally attended with the blessing of health, if not riches'. But there is no doubt the system of woollen cloth production in seventeenth- and eighteenth-century Britain

Sheep-washing in Yorkshire, early 1900s, postcard.

SHEEP WASHING

did provide work and income for entire areas, especially in the North, and in ways that engaged whole households. This was because the techniques and technologies used were not very different from those of medieval and even ancient times.

That, however, was about to change. Within a century, the populous and lively villages that delighted Defoe were extensively depopulated. The Industrial Revolution had begun, and it had done so in the wool and cotton manufacturing districts of the north of England. Innovations in spinning and weaving had occurred that would utterly transform the economy, the social structure and the environment of Britain – and the rest of the world.

In 1733 John Kaye applied for a patent for 'a new engine or machine for opening and dressing wool'. His 'Flying Shuttle' allowed the weaver, instead of manually passing the shuttle carrying the cross-thread (weft) across the horizontal threads (warp) on the loom, to activate a device that threw the shuttle back and forth mechanically. This allowed 'one weaver to work two and half times as fast as on a handloom' and expanded the potential dimensions of the material thereby produced, 'since the width

A spinning jenny.

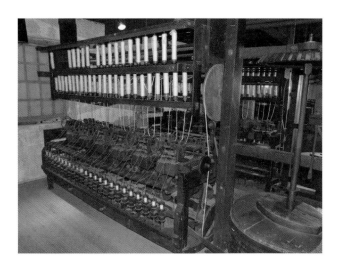

Water frame.

of the cloth no longer depended on the physical reach of the weaver'.[3] Now, however, the speed of weaving was held back by the pace at which yarn could be supplied to the loom, so the next step was the creation, by Thomas Highs and James Hargreaves, of the 'Spinning Jenny', a machine that allowed one person to operate eight spindles simultaneously. Highs followed this with a faster version, powered by water, called the 'Water Frame'.

The names of these ingenious inventors, however, are far less well known than that of Richard Arkwright, a man credited with being one of the founders of the Industrial Revolution. He gained this place in history by adopting the new inventions – not, in all cases, with due acknowledgement of their originators – and combining them with borrowed capital to create the first mechanized mills during the 1770s. Their success, and his consequent and considerable wealth, were due not only to the unprecedented efficiency of automated production but to Arkwright's use of child labour and his imposition of extremely long working hours.

Heaton woollen mills, Bradford, 1860.

Although these first mechanized mills were for cotton production, wool mills soon followed, emulating both the technology and the employment practices established by Arkwright.

In their initial form, because they were driven by waterwheels, mechanized mills had to be located beside rivers, but the development of coal-fired steam engines soon freed them from that restriction. The first such engine was installed in a textile mill in 1783. By the end of the century, fully automated mills were all over the North of England. Industrial cities based on textile production began to spread exponentially: Manchester increased its population by 1,000 per cent in the first half of the nineteenth century. The new urban working class who laboured in the mills derived, of course, from the districts described a century earlier by Defoe, whose spinning wheels and hand-looms were now obsolete. By 1837 William Youatt could write that woollen manufacture, 'early and unequivocally acknowledged to be the foundation of national prosperity and wealth', should be estimated as 'employing nearly 350,000 individuals, and ultimately yielding manufactures to the amount of at least twenty-one millions of pounds annually'.[4]

By this time, British wool production had come to rely centrally on the finer fleeces, especially from merinos, imported from overseas – hence the mutual impetus given by industrialization to colonialism and vice versa. Meanwhile, Britain's sheep population continued to supply heavier and longer wools, but the main part of it was now put to another use altogether. The urban districts that grew up around the mills were inhabited by workers who no longer – as they had when they produced cloth manually in rural villages – farmed their own food. The result was a fast-expanding urban demand for meat, which, combined with the sinking

William Wyld, *View of Manchester from Kersal Moor*, 1852, watercolour.

117

demand for British-grown fleeces, resulted in a swift and drastic metamorphosis for certain breeds of sheep. They were reinvented as meat-producing machines: fat, heavy and solid; blocks of flesh on legs.

What we would call scientific experimentation in sheep-breeding was already sufficiently well recognized in the earlier part of the eighteenth century for Jonathan Swift to mock it in *Gulliver's Travels* (1726). During his third voyage, Gulliver visits a satirically topsy-turvy version of the Royal Society, where he meets one of the foremost 'Advancers of speculative Learning', who is attempting,

> by a certain Composition of Gums, Minerals, and Vegetables outwardly applied, to prevent the Growth of Wool upon young Lambs; and he hoped in a reasonable time to propagate the Breed of naked Sheep all over the Kingdom.[5]

This experiment occurs amid a whole range of wrong-headed endeavours (including attempts to derive sunlight from cucumbers, and to reverse-process 'ordure' back into food), and in this case, the tenor of the joke depends upon Swift's inability to imagine what point there could possibly be in naked sheep – because, at the time of writing, just a few years before Defoe's visit to Yorkshire's West Riding, sheep were still synonymous with wool production. By the end of the century, the satirical point would be lost because breeders were hard at work producing sheep whose wool production was either irrelevant or secondary to their meat yield.[6]

The New or Dishley Leicester (or Leicestershire), selectively bred by Robert Bakewell in the middle of the eighteenth century, is 'often described as the first viable offspring of modern industrial livestock breeding'; Franklin calls it 'the first modern breed of sheep'.[7] Robert Trow-Smith describes the New Leicester as a 'butcher's sheep for cutting up for mutton for the masses'.[8] With its barrel body and short legs, the new sheep was 'considered revolutionary and astonishing', especially since Bakewell claimed 'to have designed and reshaped this fast maturing animal in his mind before bringing it into existence. It was as though an engineer had invented a new machine.'[9]

'The superior qualities of the Leicestershire breed', wrote Thomas Bewick in his authoritative *General History of Quadrupeds* (1790), 'are, that they will feed quickly fat at almost any age, even on indifferent pastures, and carry the greatest quantity of mutton upon the smallest bone'. He also praised Bakewell's highly profitable system for charging stud fees to other farmers: 'the modern practice of letting out Rams for hire by the season . . . is likely, for some time, to prove a copious source of wealth to the country at large.'[10]

In addition, Bewick documented the achievements of other breeders, reserving particular praise for the stock-farmers of Tees-water, who, 'by persevering in the same laudable plan of improvement so successfully begun by the late Mr Bakewell . . . have produced a kind which is looked upon by judges as nearly approaching to perfection.' Sheep of this variety, the Tees-water Improved, 'possess the thriving or fattening quality of the Dishley [New Leicester] breed, and are fit for the butcher at as early an age'. One paragon of this breed proved, upon slaughter, to weigh 'sixty-two pounds ten ounces per quarter, avoirdupois; a circumstance never before heard of in this island', while the 'extraordinary fecundity' of the 'improved' ewes allows them to bear as many as five lambs at a time.[11]

On the page facing his picture of the Tees-water Improved, Bewick portrays the Tees-water Old or Unimproved, 'for the purpose of shewing its uncouth and uncultivated appearance, in contrast to those of the improved kind'.[12] To the eye of the

W. H. Davis,
Mr Healey's Sheep,
1838, oil on canvas.

non-farmer, the effect of this comparison is quite different. The variable contours of the 'unimproved' Tees-water – the slight concavity in the middle of the spine and the convexity of the belly, the bulges of muscle at flank and shoulder, the strong forward-thrust neck, the distinction between forehead and muzzle, the large eyes – give the figure a vitality and grace lacking in its 'improved' descendant, from whose body all contours have been smoothed away by the addition of extra flesh: the spine, from tail-base to skull, is dead straight, and matched below by a nearly straight line from abdomen to chest; the perpendicular curves of chest and buttocks at either end complete the transformation of the animal into a rectangle with rounded corners. The legs have become mere stalks for holding up this blank slab of meat, and the head on its shortened neck is reduced to a small, geometrically regular triangle, devoid of expression, resembling a spigot through which grass can be fed for processing into mutton.

The 'Unimproved'
(bottom) and
'Improved'
(top) Tees-water
breed, wood
engravings from
Thomas Bewick's
*General History of
Quadrupeds* (1790).

For the sheep 'improvers' of the eighteenth and nineteenth centuries, the transformation of living animals into walking meat-packs became a matter of boastful pride. Bewick's Tees-water Improved looks relatively lively and natural in comparison with some of the animals in the paintings that breeders and farmers commissioned to celebrate their prize stock lines. Perhaps the most alarming is W. H. Davis's *Mr Healey's Sheep* (1838). Here the animal's body has been even further distorted – the spine is now convex rather than straight, and the whole shape seems to be slipping sideways under its own weight, transforming Bewick's rounded rectangle into a top-heavy parallelogram. Moreover, the overall size of the animal is exaggerated (at least one hopes so!): the sheep has become, in proportion to its owner – who is shown trying to stuff it even fuller with turnips – the size of an ox.

A more realistic technique is typical of James Ward, who was a member of the Royal Academy and considered the greatest animal painter of the first half of the nineteenth century. 'Commissioned by the Board of Agriculture to undertake 200 paintings of all the native breeds of domestic livestock', Ward 'visited many of the most successful breeders of the day'. Rather than deploying the hyperbolic scale and distorted contours seen in the Davies picture, Ward nevertheless ensured his models were as large as possible by painting animals that, 'having already reached the peak of their condition . . . were destined for immi-nent slaughter, requiring him to work all night by candlelight before they were dispatched the following morning'.[13]

It is intensely ironic – though by no means coincidental – that the same historical moment that produced industrialized wool manufacture and the 'perfect' mutton-producing breed also gave rise to one of the purest literary evocations of the sheep as a symbol of natural and spiritual innocence. In 1794 the painter and poet William Blake printed his *Songs of Innocence and*

Experience, two linked collections of poems illuminated by his own visionary engravings. One of the more famous poems, 'The Lamb', typifies the childlike but mysteriously potent qualities of the work as a whole:

> Little lamb who made thee
> Dost thou know who made thee
> Gave thee life & bid thee feed.
> By the stream & o'er the mead;
> Gave thee clothing of delight.
> Softest clothing wooly bright;
> Gave thee such a tender voice.
> Making all the vales rejoice:
> Little lamb, who made thee
> Dost thou know who made thee
>
> Little lamb I'll tell thee,
> Little lamb I'll tell thee;
> He is called by thy name,
> For he calls himself a Lamb:
> He is meek & he is mild,
> He became a little child:
> I a child & thou a lamb,
> We are called by his name,
> Little Lamb, God bless thee,
> Little Lamb, God bless thee.[14]

At first, the poem seems no more than a pious nursery rhyme, something designed to teach a Christian lesson to young children. (Indeed it was originally intended to be sung.) But the deceptively simple structure – two stanzas of couplets following a question-and-answer format – depends on a slightly surprising

William Blake's poem 'The Lamb', from *Songs of Innocence and of Experience* (1789), relief and white-line etching with hand colouring.

mode of address: it is the child who speaks, addressing the lamb, telling the story of Jesus. By this means, with increasing intensity, the poem concentrates into the apparently bland figure of the lamb three highly potent representations of innocence: the 'soft' and 'tender' young animal itself; the 'little child' who speaks;

and Jesus, who is at once creator, Christ-child, Lamb of God and Good Shepherd.

More than this, when placed within the context of the overall collection, 'The Lamb' generates a whole set of other correspondences and tensions because, in a way typical of Blake, it operates as part of a larger system of contraries. The poems in the first book of the collection, 'Songs of Innocence', are paired against those in 'Experience': the opposite number of 'The Lamb' is 'The Tyger'. Here the same question is asked of a very different animal, and in a very different poetic voice. The childlike question, 'Dost thou know who made thee', with its reassuringly immediate answer, has become a complex, abstract, anxious and adult expression of cosmic doubt. 'What immortal hand or eye, / Dare frame thy fearful symmetry?' asks the speaker, and later, 'Did he who made the Lamb make thee?' In additional contrast, the pastoral and rural provenance of the lamb – who is given life and sustenance

James Ward,
A Border Leicester Ewe, c. 1795,
oil on canvas.

'by the stream & o'er the mead', and given a 'tender voice' to make 'all the vales rejoice' – stands in stark opposition to the 'hammer' 'chain' and 'furnace' that the later poem associates with the making of the tiger. The tiger seems here like a product of manufacture, a kind of nightmarish industrial machine.[15]

In a related fashion, in his later 'prophetic' works, Blake draws on imagery derived from industrial wool production to produce his darkest and most scathing evocations of contemporary life and thought. 'Behold the Loom of Locke', Blake writes in *Jerusalem*, 'whose Woof rages dire / Washed by the water-wheels of Newton.' The rationalist philosophies of Blake's *bêtes noires*, John Locke and Isaac Newton, are described as 'cruel Works / Of many Wheels . . . with cogs tyrannic / Moving by compulsion each Other', producing a black cloth that 'in heavy wreathes folds over every Nation'.[16] Throughout his writing, in order to evoke the spiritual and material crises of his time, Blake returns to these two contrary archetypes of the relationship between human and sheep. On the one hand, he repeatedly embodies spiritual innocence through the figures of lamb and shepherd and pastoral nature; on the other, he evokes the exploitative, cruel, enslaving and despoiling aspects of industrialization using terrifying images drawn from the technology of the mechanized wool mill: blanketing smoke, demonically whirring looms, compulsively grinding cogs. These contraries exemplify two related aspects fundamental to the Romantic reaction against industrial modernity, which still infuse the environmental movements to this day: nostalgia for the garden and mistrust of the machine.

For actual sheep in industrial societies, the last two centuries have mostly involved a movement further from the garden and closer to the machine. It is sometimes assumed that today's sheep are more fortunate than other livestock farmed on a large scale, in that they are pastured in the open rather than in the

William Hogarth, *The Second Stage of Cruelty*, 1751, printed engraving. Tom Nero has progressed from torturing a dog to beating a horse, while beside him a drover beats his sheep. The next stage will be robbery, seduction and murder.

factory farming systems – the battery farms, feedlots, sow crates, farrowing stalls and 'Concentrated Animal Feeding Operations' – to which chickens, cattle, pigs and many other species are subjected by the billion. Yet the reality is not so reassuring.

In the first place, even though sheep are mostly still raised on pastures, the very large scale on which pastoralism occurs encourages practices that have extremely adverse implications for the animals. In New Zealand, ewes are routinely forced into early ovulation in order that they bear lambs in August, so farmers can supply to meat companies in advance of their competitors. In many

Angela Singer, *Chilled Lamb*, taxidermied body of an early lamb who died of hypothermia, decorated with jewelled blowflies, 2001. This piece was purchased by Sir James Wallace, the owner of New Zealand's largest meat-rendering business.

parts of the country, however, heavy snowfalls and extended icy conditions can occur well into September and beyond – especially in the south and the high country districts where most sheep are farmed. As a result, about one-tenth of lambs in the major pastoral districts of Southland and West Otago die from exposure every year. In general terms, New Zealand farmers are lax in providing shelter: during the severe snows of 1992, 50 per cent of all sheep in the Canterbury region died of exposure, stress, starvation or drowning – 4,000 on one farm alone.[17]

Apart from slaughter itself, and rough handling during shearing and transport, the most brutal practice routinely carried out among sheep in New Zealand and Australia is mulesing, so called after John Mules, the farmer who invented the technique. Because the skin of merinos has been selectively bred to grow loose and wrinkly (to increase the area available for yielding wool), they are especially prone to the buildup of faecal matter around the anus, and therefore to fly-strike, the infected infestation of eggs and maggots from blowflies in matted wool. Fly-strike can be effectively prevented, even in merinos, by regular 'crutching' (trimming of the wool around the anus), washing, vaccination or 'drenching' (dosing with pesticides). However, since merinos are farmed in very numerous flocks and on vast stations with many remote pastures, farmers find it more cost-effective to practise mulesing, which involves flaying the skin, most often without anaesthetic, from a wide area surrounding the anus, thereby supposedly preventing the growth of matted wool that would be susceptible to fly-strike. It requires only a moment's reflection to imagine what this procedure – and its aftermath – must feel like. For those lacking, or suspicious of, imaginative sympathy, there is empirical evidence. A series of studies has shown that mulesed lambs feel intense pain after the procedure, and avoid the handler who performs it for some weeks. More-over, 35 per cent of mulesed sheep still suffer from fly-strike. Nevertheless, according to animal advocates, half of the merino sheep in New Zealand are still subject to mulesing, along with 20 million per year in Australia.[18]

Farmers in both countries also routinely practise the follow-ing procedures without pain relief: tail docking (amputating the tail with a rubber ring or hot iron), pizzle dropping (cutting the skin that joins the penis to the belly in order to avoid pizzle rot) and castration. In all cases, again, studies have shown that the animals experience long periods of trauma and pain following these procedures.[19]

As for 'factory farming': almost all sheep will suffer the con-ditions of concentrated confinement for at least the last few days of their lives – and many millions for much longer than that – during transport to slaughter or live export overseas. Considerable stress results from mustering and loading into trucks (a process involving the use of dogs, electric prods and stock canes). Once they are on board, the animals endure travel – often over the course of days – without food or water, in an environment in which dense crowding produces soaring temperatures and ammonia buildup from waste. On arrival at the slaughterhouse sheep may be kept in 'lairage' – crowded into bare concrete yards, without food – for 24 hours prior to slaughter.

The slaughter process itself, in its conventional form, entails initial stunning of the animal using a penetrating captive bolt or an electrical charge: the latter causes 'an epileptiform seizure, with immobility followed by convulsions with kicking and paddling movements'. Studies have shown that one out of every ten animals is not properly knocked out by this means and so endures slaughter in a conscious state. The usual method of slaughter is by bleeding, which involves cutting open the animal's chest to sever the anterior vena cava and the bicarotid arterial trunk.[20]

An even more intensive form of industrialized sheep farming occurs in the live export trade. Over 2 million sheep a year are exported from Australia by sea, on voyages that sometimes last several weeks, to a wide range of countries: Indonesia, Malaysia, Israel, Mexico, Japan, China and various parts of the Middle East. The conditions on board ship are as bad as for any intensive confinement system on land: sheep are kept in pens on multistorey decks with an average of 0.25 to 0.4 square metres (1 square foot) of space per animal – about as much room as would be provided by a medium to large cardboard box – for weeks on end, during which they are exposed to extremes of temperature, high winds and rough seas. The Australian government's records show half a million reported deaths during such voyages between 2000 and 2012.[21] In addition to these routine and expected mortalities, the industry has experienced many major shipboard disasters over the years. To mention only incidents resulting in many thousands of deaths at a time: in 1980, 40,000 sheep (an entire cargo) were burnt to death on a fire aboard the *Farid Fares*; in 1981, nearly 9,000 died due to ventilation problems on the *Persia*; in 1990, 10,000 died on the 'state-of-the-art' *Cormo Express*, bound from New Zealand to the Middle East, due to ventilation breakdown causing pneumonia, heatstroke and other diseases; in 1991, 30,000 died due to poor ventilation on arrival in war-devastated Kuwait; in 1995, 15,000 died from heatstroke on the *Fernanda F.*; in 1996, close to 70,000 died in a fire aboard the *Uniceb*; in 2002, a combined total of 15,000 died on four

Sue Coe, 'Mulesing', from *Sheep of Fools* (2005).

ships bound for the Middle East; in 2003, over 6,000 died aboard the *Cormo Express* (again); and in 2013, over 4,000 died on the *MV Bader III*.[22]

Sue Coe, 'The Farid Fares Burning', from *Sheep of Fools*.

Other criticisms levelled at the live export trade relate to slaughter practices in the destination countries, especially where sheep undergo halal slaughter, according to Islamic law, which requires animals to die more slowly than via conventional slaughter – most often by having their throats cut while still fully conscious, so their hearts can pump as much blood as possible from their bodies. Other instances of abuse of exported animals at their destinations have also been exposed by animal advocates. In 2012 video footage released by Animals Australia of a location in Pakistan showed the 'cull' of 22,000 recently arrived sheep suspected of infection: animals are shown 'dragged, beaten, having their throats sawn at with blunt knives, and thrown into mass graves – some of them still alive hours later'.[23]

The live export event that caused the most intensive media scrutiny – although it was far from the most catastrophic from the animals' perspective – was the voyage of the *Cormo Express*, carrying 58,000 animals, to Saudi Arabia in 2003. On the ship's arrival in Jeddah, its cargo was rejected by Saudi veterinary officials, who claimed that one-third of the flock showed signs of the viral infection scabby mouth. For two months, while the sheep were stranded aboard ship in the Persian Gulf and the mortality rate rose, the Australian government made increasingly desperate overtures to 50 other countries to take them, even offering to deliver them for free, but the suggestion of infection meant that none would accept them. Nor would Australian quarantine laws allow the ship to return home, since the animals had now been potentially exposed to exotic diseases or insects. In the end, Eritrea was paid AUS$1 million and given 3,000 tons of feed to accept the sheep – by which time more than 6,000 had died.[24]

Photographs taken during a routine day at an animal saleyard in Australia, during which 32,000 sheep were bought and sold, mostly for slaughter. The last image shows a dumpster full of animals that died during the course of the day due to stress, rough handling or dehydration. Photographs by Jo-Anne McArthur, in *We Animals* (2014).

The plight of these sheep – caught between agricultural officials at their destination, who alleged they arrived with disease, and those in their country of origin, who denied the presence of that disease but would not take them back because of possible exposure to other diseases en route – demonstrates the peculiar vulnerability of sheep to global and international regulatory regimes designed to protect agricultural economies. Many millions of sheep have died at the stroke of an official's pen. In 2001 the entire cattle and sheep industry of Great Britain was thrown into chaos by the discovery of foot-and-mouth disease in Northumberland. Within nine months, 3.8 million animals had been slaughtered to prevent the spread of the disease; and massive damage to agriculture was compounded by an estimated £10 billion of income lost by the tourist industry due to restrictions on travel in rural areas, and the concomitant discouragement of visitors to Great Britain in general. For a time, the army was required to manage the slaughter of herds suspected of infection, along with the disruption to transport, communications, villages and towns all across the country. All this was demanded, not by the threat of a potentially lethal disease, but by international regulations governing agricultural transport and exchange – for as Franklin points out, foot-and-mouth 'is harmless to humans and rarely infects them', while even to sheep it is rarely fatal, and usually 'no more severe than the common cold'. It mainly causes problems in dairy herds, where (although once again seldom lethal) it reduces milk yield; hence its economic impact, which is massively compounded by the inability of affected countries to trade with countries where the virus is absent or at least quiescent. Sheep are therefore slaughtered during a foot-and-mouth outbreak only because they can transmit unprofitability to other agricultural sectors. Foot-and-mouth disease is 'only lethal to domestic animals because it is *economically intolerable* to humans'.[25]

Sheep, then, like all livestock animals, have become increasingly subject to a range of regulatory systems, culling and slaughtering regimes, intensive confinement systems and invasive manipulations, usually proportional in severity to the scale of the late industrial global agricultural system of which they are now a highly profitable part.

They have also, like so many other species, been subject to punishing treatment at the hands of the fashion industry. The most dismaying examples are so-called Persian and broadtail lamb products. The Vintage Fashion Guild describes these respectively as follows:

the skin of the young Lamb of the Karakul breed of sheep or top-cross breed of such sheep, having hair formed in knuckled curls, [and] the skin of the prematurely born,

A ewe and her lambs are taken from a factory farm by activists from a Spanish abolitionist group, Igualdad Animal. Photograph by Jo-Anne McArthur, in *We Animals* (2014).

stillborn, or very young Lamb of the Karakul breed of sheep or top-cross breed of such sheep, having flat light-weight fur with a moiré pattern.

This website reassures ethically minded consumers that such fabrics are 'acceptable to wear in today's anti-fur society' since they are 'by-product[s] of an animal that is also a food source'.[26] But nothing could be further from the truth. Both Persian and broadtail lamb skins are produced by cutting lamb foetuses from the bodies of their mothers, which have been impregnated specifically for the purpose and then slaughtered. About 4–5 million Persian or broadtail pelts are produced for high fashion each year.[27]

Equally invisible to most people is the extent to which sheep are still today subject to scientific experimentation. Most often this is in the service of agriculture – scientists continually manipulate sheep and lambs in order to find ways of improving yields of wool or meat. A great many painful and invasive studies have been undertaken that involved deliberately infecting sheep with fly-strike and observing the effects of the consequent ammonia toxicity, in some cases to the point of death. In New Zealand, where agricultural research accounts for most of the scientific experiments on animals, around 20 per cent of the 250,000 animals used in experiments annually are sheep.[28] In Australia official statistics are provided by only half the states in the Federation, but these show as many as 37,000 sheep experimented upon per year.[29] In both countries, the procedures routinely undertaken on sheep include 'cut and paste' manipulations, in which the live animal's belly is cut open and sections of the intestine are pulled out and kept external to the body for extended periods in order that parasites can be introduced to the gut and observed; lethal infestation of lambs with parasites; and 'shock and burn' tests to measure 'aversion' to pain.[30]

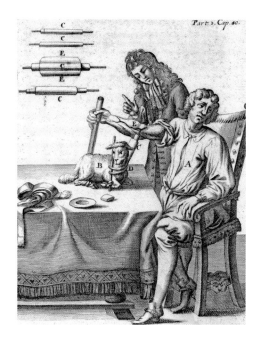

Early blood
transfusion from
a lamb to a man,
1705.

There has also been, at least since the birth of the modern
scientific method in the seventeenth century, a tradition of experi-
menting on sheep as proxies for humans. This way of using sheep
– an updated version of their ancient sacrificial role – exemplifies
the paradox often identified by critics of animal experimentation:
on the one hand, sheep are considered similar enough to humans
that what is discovered in them may be applicable to us; on the
other, they are assumed to be sufficiently different that invasive,
excruciating and lethal procedures may be carried out without
ethical constraint.

In 1667 the French physician Jean-Baptiste Denys and the
Englishman Richard Lower each claimed to have performed the
first cross-species blood transfusion involving a human. Denys

gave blood from a lamb to a young man suffering from a fever; Lower gave sheep's blood to a Cambridge University student who was 'cracked a little in the head'.[31] In Thomas Shadwell's *The Virtuoso* (1676), which satirizes the experiments conducted by members of the Royal Society in the name of the 'New Science', a transfusion of sheep's blood into a man's body produces a rapid change in disposition: 'the Patient from being Maniacal, or raging mad, became wholly Ovine or Sheepish; he bleated perpetually, and chew'd the Cud.'[32]

Between the seventeenth and twenty-first centuries, sheep have often been used in experiments designed to advance human medical treatments: lambs have been shaken to death by scientists interested in human 'shaken baby syndrome'; artificially inseminated ewes have been encouraged to overeat, and they and their lambs subsequently dissected, to investigate the effects of obesity on human mothers and babies; pregnant ewes have been injected with alcohol and then dissected to find out what kinds of foetal abnormalities result and whether these have applications to humans.[33]

By far the most famous scientific experiment involving a sheep, though, was the use of cloning technology at the Roslin Institute in Edinburgh in 1996 to create a ewe named Dolly. The scientists responsible explained their choice of name: 'Dolly is derived from a mammary gland cell and we couldn't think of a more impressive pair of glands than Dolly Parton's.'[34] This clumsy piece of lab-culture wit has some distasteful implications, considering the thoroughness and thoughtlessness with which female bodies, human and non-human alike, have been manipulated over the course of scientific history.

It is popularly assumed that Dolly's significance lies in being the first cloned animal. In fact, the first animals cloned by human manipulation were tadpoles, during the 1950s. Sheep were the first

Dolly poses –
posthumously –
with her creator,
Professor Ian
Wilmut.

mammals cloned, but that, too, was achieved before Dolly, during the 1980s. What made Dolly unprecedented was that she was cloned from an adult cell, rather than (as in previous clonings) from an embryonic stem cell. This was innovative because it had previously been taken as axiomatic that 'once cells are committed to the tasks of adulthood, they cannot again be totipotent' (that is, they cannot differentiate into other cell types). The team at Roslin, however, by means of nuclear transfer of genetic material, succeeded in 'reprogramming' a cell from an 'almost elderly' ewe so that it could behave like an embryonic cell and produce a new animal.[35]

Evidently aware – or perhaps having been made aware – of the potential for their enterprise to be publicly perceived as dangerously profane, the scientists who produced Dolly engaged in a public relations campaign designed to make their achievement both understandable and acceptable to a wide audience. To combat the conventional fear that biotechnology (especially cloning) shows disrespect for individual lives, they were at pains to express how much personal affection they felt for Dolly. 'People think I wouldn't miss her because I could make another Dolly', said Ian Wilmut, one of the chief scientists responsible for the project, 'but what they don't understand is that she has her own individuality and there would never be another sheep like her.'[36] Roslin also distributed a photograph of the smiling Wilmut with his arm around Dolly – which, however, seems ambiguous to say the least when we realize it was taken posthumously, using her taxidermied body, which is kept on display at the Institute.

A rather different problem emerges in the book that Wilmut and his colleague Keith Campbell wrote with the popular science writer Colin Tudge to appeal to a general audience. In that volume, the authors' stated fondness for Dolly quickly transforms into exorbitant admiration for their own genius. Their description of her as 'the most extraordinary creature ever to be born' and the title they chose for their book – *The Second Creation* (2000) – are hardly likely to mitigate the common perception that scientists can develop god complexes. Further on, with no apparent awareness of their own grandiosity, Wilmut and Campbell assess their achievement as follows: 'All in all, Dolly is the stuff of which myths are made. Her birth was otherworldly, literally a virgin birth . . .

Gregor Kregar, *Matthew 12:12:* a gallery installation in two parts, including live sheep in coloured woollen jackets penned outside and a mob of model sheep inside. Christchurch Art Gallery, New Zealand, 2006.

The scientific magi were suitably amazed.' The technology that produced Dolly, they go on to explain, 'will offer our successors a degree of control over life's processes that will come effectively to seem absolute'.[37]

As well as comparing their achievements favourably with those of God, Dolly's progenitors are explicit about the financial dimension of their work. As Franklin points out, projects like the creation of Dolly, for all their rhetoric about improving human life, are part of the broader capitalist enterprise that has made *Ovis aries* so readily convertible into resources, assets, investments, commodities and profits for thousands of years. Franklin aptly describes Dolly as a very particular kind of hybrid: 'the offspring of "pure science" crossed with venture capital'. The cloning projects at Roslin were funded by a private company, PPL Therapeutics, whose share price doubled overnight when Dolly's creation was announced. And when the exclusive licence to the Dolly patents was sold to an American private enterprise, Geron Corporation, that company's stock price immediately rose by one-third.[38]

Little lamb, who made thee? Little lamb, I'll tell thee.

6 Sheepliness

The Egyptians worshipped them, the Romans dressed them in fitted coats, the Christians made them synonymous with their divine saviour. In Homer's *Odyssey*, the Cyclops Polyphemus sought sympathy from his favourite wether; the English farmer Thomas Tryon did his best to understand the language of bleating; the Romantic poet William Blake favourably compared the little lamb with an innocent child and with Jesus himself. Throughout the 11,000 years of history shared by our two species, some people have thought very highly of sheep. Yet this tendency has been massively outweighed by another tradition, which has had far greater impact on the lives of actual sheep. According to this tradition, sheep are negligible in themselves, but valuable insofar as they can be treated as a mass of raw material, to be used in whatever way yields the most benefit and profit to humans. In this final chapter, I will survey some examples of how these different tendencies – face-to-face encounter, idealization and exploitation – have manifested in portrayals of sheep in folklore, popular culture and the arts. In this way, I'll attempt to return, in the light of the history of human–ovine relations traced in the preceding chapters, to the issues raised at the start of this book.

One of the few legends in which sheep play an active role describes how the druids of King Cormac, the third-century High King of Ireland, sent out three brown sheep to attack the enemy

Collection of sheep
paraphernalia.

forces during his campaign against the province of Munster. The latter were, perhaps understandably, underwhelmed by this tactic – until the sheep got close enough to make visible their hard, bony heads, their horny skins and noses made of iron. When they arrived, it became apparent that Cormac's battle-sheep also had 'the swiftness of the swallow, the agility of the weasel, the rapidity of birds', and each one proved equal to a hundred warriors. They were, in fact, three transformed druidesses, and could only be defeated by answering magic from the Munster druid, who created three fire-breathing dogs to set the monstrous sheeps' fleeces aflame.[1]

The central dynamic of this tale, of course, is that the Munster army's assumptions about sheepish harmlessness permit the weaponized sheep to get close enough to be lethal; their offensive power is inversely proportionate to the presumed inoffensiveness of their species. Equally clearly, the Munster druid's response is a kind of joke at the expense of sheep – all he needs to put them back in their place is a pack of similarly monstrous sheepdogs. In these ways, the story demonstrates a pattern that pervades most popular narratives about sheep: the stereotype of dull passivity, although it may sometimes be surprisingly challenged, is almost always ultimately reinforced.

Nowhere is the theme of ovine passivity more vividly expressed than in a legend from *The Travels of Sir John Mandeville*, a popular fourteenth-century travelogue, which describes how in the Far East

> there groweth a manner of fruit, as though it were gourds. And when they be ripe, men cut them a-two, and men find within a little beast, in flesh, in bone, and blood, as though it were a little lamb without wool. And men eat both the fruit and the beast.[2]

This curious organism, variously known as the Barometz or the Vegetable Lamb of Tartary, occurs rather differently in the Talmudic tradition, which describes the lamb attached by its navel to a stem rooted in the earth. Once the lamb consumes all the grass within reach of its tether, the stem withers and the creature dies.[3] During the Enlightenment the existence of the vegetable lamb became the subject of expert debate. In 1781 the poet-naturalist Erasmus Darwin (grandfather of Charles) described the species in one of his long zoological poems, though he imagined the creature implanted through her legs rather than her navel:

Rooted in earth each cloven foot descends,
And round and round her flexile neck she bends . . .
Eyes with mute tenderness her distant dam,
Or seems to bleat, a *vegetable lamb*.[4]

What seems remarkable here is less that the story of the vegetable lamb was ever believed – in fact it was just as often treated with scepticism as with credulity – but that it became so popular during the very centuries in which Europeans were developing the most advanced and extensive sheep-rearing culture in history. Imagining *Ovis* as an animal so completely passive that it can be plucked from a tree like ripe fruit appealed, it would seem, to a culture dependent for its prosperity and power on harvesting sheep in vast numbers.

In 1887 the scholar Henry Lee concluded that the vegetable lamb story derived from European travellers' descriptions of the cotton plant. He cited as evidence the words of Herodotus, who referred to trees that 'bear for their fruit fleeces surpassing those of sheep' from which warm clothing could be made.[5] That seems conclusive, but the legend had a surprising coda. A couple of decades earlier, pastoralists in New Zealand had discovered an

Vegetable Lamb of Tartary, from *The Travels of Sir John Mandeville*, 14th century.

Barometz, from Claude Duret's *Histoire Admirable des Plantes* (1605).

Vegetable sheep (*Raoulia*) in Canterbury, New Zealand.

antipodean species of vegetable ovine. *Haastia pulvinaris* and *Raoulia eximia*, endemic to the alpine regions of New Zealand's South Island, are mat plants belonging to the daisy family, with cushion-forming leaves densely covered in tawny or grey-white hairs. Lying in clumps a metre or two in diameter among rocks and scree, they vividly justify their popular names: vegetable sheep and sheep plant.[6] On first encountering *Haastia* and *Raoulia*, Victorian naturalists responded with a characteristic blend of astonishment, calculation and disdain. 'Although singular and interesting to the botanist', wrote John R. Jackson, curator of the Museum at the Royal Gardens in Kew, in 1867,

> these plants are of no value economically, but, on the contrary . . . certain species of them are a plague to the shepherds, inasmuch as they give them much trouble and annoyance to discern between an animal sheep and a vegetable sheep.[7]

Realistically, it seems unlikely that shepherds would have genuine
difficulty telling alpine mat plants apart from sheep. More probably, the idea of vegetable sheep survives simply because it
continues to amuse in societies with pastoral economies, where
associating sheep with passivity and stupidity is the most com-
fortable attitude to adopt while farming them in ways that inhibit
their expression of those forms of social intelligence endemic to
their kind.

Two recent examples from popular culture demonstrate this
continued link between pastoralism and the denigration of sheep.
In 2006 the comedy horror film *Black Sheep* (dir. Jonathan King)
imagined a scenario in which, to quote the movie's tagline, 'an

experiment in genetic engineering turns harmless sheep into blood-thirsty killers that terrorize a sprawling New Zealand farm'. At first glance, this might seem a departure from the conventional associations of sheepishness: animals so herbivorous they are virtually part of the vegetable kingdom transform into man-eaters. But of course the film only works because the conventional view of sheep is so ingrained in the first place. The filmmakers know the audience will laugh at the ludicrous reversal of that docile typecasting. The best example of this strategy – and the funniest moment in the film – is when the main characters react with exaggerated terror as a flock of (evidently ordinary and harmless) sheep trots down a slope in their direction – a kind of reversal of Cormac's ovine drone attack.

Something similar – an apparent challenge to the stereotype of sheepishness, which turns out to reinforce it – occurred in 2004, when a merino wether from Bendigo Station in New Zealand's South Island became a media celebrity after avoiding the shearers for six years. His media minders named him Shrek, after the lovable ogre of the animated films. The shearing of his 27-kg (60-lb) fleece was broadcast live on national television and, even more oddly, re-enacted two years later, for the self-promotion of the sheep's owner, on an iceberg that had drifted unusually close to New Zealand's southern coast. His profile continued to flourish as he became the subject of children's stories and coffee-table books. Like the film *Black Sheep* – and like the idiom from which that title comes, according to which the black sheep is the maverick who goes against the flock[8] – Shrek might seem to have contradicted conventional assumptions about sheepish lack of initiative and individualism. As it turned out, however, like both the film and the idiom, he functioned as an exception that proves the rule. The media response to Shrek made very clear that he was noteworthy only because he rose above the conformist

Shrek the sheep.

passivity considered typical of his species; he resisted human control, separated himself from his flock and became an individual and hence worthy of respect. In the process, the belief that most sheep *aren't like that* was powerfully reinforced. (In fact, 'hermit sheep' who evade muster are quite common; it's just that most of them don't have PR agents.)

Indeed, mockery of Shrek's supposed uniqueness and intimations of his 'real' sheepish status and proper destiny were never far from the surface. When television cameras captured Shrek's meeting on the steps of Parliament with New Zealand's Prime Minister at the time, Helen Clark, one reporter asked how this photo opportunity compared with the lamb dinner she had served the visiting president of Chile the evening before. Some time later, a TV satire screened a story that claimed to break the news of Shrek's slaughter, due to 'clerical error', in a 'routine home kill'. 'Secretly obtained footage' showed a merino draped in a red cape emblazoned with the name Shrek, dragged from his flock-mates, slaughtered and skinned, while the voiceover parodied the language of media sensation:

> this afternoon, the stellar career of the world's most recognisable sheep came to an abrupt end . . . After spending a few final moments with friends, the former Prime-Ministerial confidant [was] taken aside and led to a custom-built killing shed. With his trademark jacket still draped round his soon-to-be-slit neck like a superhero's cape . . . under the gaze of our cameras, the maverick merino was martyred.[9]

Following the broadcast, anxious online discussants were re-assured that the piece had been a hoax – not from the point of view of the Shrek ring-in, who was actually slaughtered, but in

Concept art by Weta Workshop for the horror film *Black Sheep* (2006).

the sense that the real Shrek was still living in luxury. The point was well made: in the eyes of most New Zealanders, Shrek remained indistinguishable from any other merino wether draped in a red cape; nor was there anything that distinguished him from the millions of his conspecifics who are routinely slaughtered, other than a media-created myth that anointed him for special treatment.

This pattern of contrasting supposed sheepish passivity and silliness with sheeply adventurousness and initiative is more enjoyably embodied in the Aardman Animations stop-motion animated series *Shaun the Sheep*. The show portrays the adventures of a flock of Suffolks – one of the most attractive of the common sheep breeds, with their white fleeces, black faces and feet, and black, rabbit-like ears. Shaun, the leader of the flock, is far cleverer than any of the human characters, and while some of his flock-mates are somewhat dim, they are anything but dull: they may stand passively on all fours munching grass while the farmer is nearby, but as soon as he is out of sight, they jump onto two legs and create havoc. Of course, once again the joke depends on the presumed incongruity of imagining sheep being so audacious – and on the amusement of seeing them return to their pasture in the nick of time so they can be back on all fours, blankly munching, just as the farmer appears. Nevertheless, like all Aardman productions, *Shaun the Sheep* probably succeeds in leaving children with the sense that there's more going on with animals than fatuous adults realize.

Cormac's battlesheep, the ovine zombies of *Black Sheep*, Shrek the maverick merino and Shaun the stop-motion Suffolk: these are all, within their respective genres of legend, cinema, news media and TV, exceptions proving the rule. Sheep are almost never considered sufficiently interesting to be the focus of popular narratives (unlike dogs, chickens and pigs, for instance, or wild animals). The same is true of the arts, where the presence of sheep is inversely proportional to their presence in history. In literature, although writers as diverse and significant as Homer, Catullus, Thomas More, William Shakespeare, Miguel de Cervantes, William Blake, Thomas Hardy and Mary Hunter Austin have registered the presence of sheep as part of the texture of everyday life, they have each tended to keep the animals themselves in the background. In the works of these writers, sheep occur incidentally, or, when they do come briefly into focus, in ways that quickly transform them from animals into something else: in Homer, into textiles or sacrificial victims; in Shakespeare, into capital; in Cervantes, into a fantasy army; in Blake, into symbols of innocence; in Hardy, into embodiments of the pastoral estate; in Austin, into wool or mutton. For the modernists of the twentieth century, similarly, on the rare occasions when sheep appear, they tend to function emblematically. Works such as Samuel Beckett's novel *Molloy* (1951) and Janet Frame's short story 'Two Sheep' (1963) and her novel *Intensive Care* (1971) all use the contrast between the naive idealization of the Arcadian tradition and the brutal realities of the slaughterhouse to portray the illusory absurdity and horror of modern human life.[10] In these cases, again, sheep are little more than allegorical figures, and inextricable from the long and dominant cultural tradition of Western ovine symbolism.

One writer who succeeds in stepping outside this tradition is Haruki Murakami, whose novel *A Wild Sheep Chase* (originally published in Japanese in 1982) is to sheep what *Moby-Dick* is to whales. Both novels concern the monomaniacal hunt for one particular and peculiarly marked animal among the multitudes of its kind. (Murakami makes the comparison explicit at one point.) Both novels, with pervasive irony but also with a sense of wonder, explore how the species they depict are exploited both for commercial profit and for symbolic meaning-making. And in

Shaun the sheep and his flock-mates, Aardman Animations, 2007.

each novel, the elusive white animal at the centre of the quest becomes invested with an ultimately sublime significance: Ishmael calls Moby-Dick 'the gliding great demon of the seas of life'; Murakami's narrator is told that an encounter with the sheep he seeks is like a connection to 'a dynamo manifesting the vital force at the root of all life in one solitary point of the universe'.[11]

The narrator of *A Wild Sheep Chase* is sent an apparently unremarkable photograph of grazing sheep, which he thoughtlessly reproduces on a prospectus for an insurance company. The image catches the attention of a shadowy right-wing organization, and our hero finds himself caught up in the search for one of the sheep in the picture, distinguishable (on close examination) by a star-shaped mark on its fleece. Murakami is a writer who draws extensively on Western cultural sources as well as Japanese ones; his novels are full of canny engagement with European and American literature, film, music and popular culture. This is certainly true of *A Wild Sheep Chase* – except when it comes to sheep, whose Western associations the novel ignores almost entirely. The Judaeo-Christian link between sheep and sacrifice, or the biblical connotations of Christ as the Lamb of God and the Good Shepherd, are absent. Instead, the mysterious star-marked sheep turns out to be a kind of possessing spirit, which enters the living bodies of individual human beings and drives them to fulfil extraordinary destinies. One character who has experienced this tells the narrator that

> In parts of Northern China and Mongol territory . . . it's believed that a sheep entering the body is a blessing from the gods. For instance, in one book published in the Yuan dynasty it's written that a 'star-bearing white sheep' entered the body of Genghis Khan.[12]

Another reason Murakami can eschew the vast weight of Western sheepish associations is the relative rareness and insignificance of sheep and sheep-farming in his native country. As another character informs the narrator, sheep were only introduced to Japan during the mid-nineteenth century. Consequently,

> few Japanese had ever seen a sheep or understood what one was . . . it might as well have been an imaginary creature on the order of a dragon or phoenix . . . Even today, Japanese know precious little about sheep. Which is to say that sheep as an animal have no historical connection with the daily

life of the Japanese. Sheep were imported at the state level from America, raised briefly, then promptly ignored.[13]

Hence, just as Murakami's sheep are largely free of Judaeo-Christian associations, they are also unencumbered by the historical and everyday familiarity that results, in Western cultures, from the pervasive influence of eleven millennia of pastoralism. Accordingly, when Murakami's narrator encounters live sheep for the first time, he has no preconceptions. Rather than perceiving them as dull, stupid or passive, or as archetypal sacrificial victims, he is struck by their uncanny and potent mindfulness:

> The instant I entered the sheep house, all two hundred sheep turned in my direction. Half the sheep stood, the other half lay on the hay spread over their pen floors. Their eyes were an unnatural blue, looking like tiny wellsprings flowing from the sides of their faces. They shone like glass eyes which reflected light from straight on. They stared at me. Not one budged. A few continued munching away on the grass in their mouth, but there was no other sound. A few, their heads protruding from their pens, had stopped drinking water and had frozen in place, fixing their eyes on me. They seemed to think as a group . . . [They] neither rejected nor accepted my presence, regarding me more as a temporary manifestation.[14]

There is nothing unbelievable in this description of how sheep might respond to a sudden human intruder. Even the glowing blue eyes are realistic. Murakami carefully describes how, in the dimly lit shed, the rays of the setting sun enter the windows, and this explains the luminous eyes. Like many animals (although not primates), sheep have a layer of reflective cells (the tapetum lucidum) behind the retina which, by reflecting light back into the eye, enhances night vision. This produces the effect of 'eye-shine' when light catches the animal's eye in a dim environment: in dogs and cats, eye-shine is usually green; in rodents and birds, red; in sheep and horses, blue.[15] The sheep confronting Murakami's narrator are thus described very accurately, in biological and etho-logical terms; they are not transformed into symbols or anthro-pomorphized. Yet they will not recede into the background either. And although they do nothing but stare at him motionlessly, the narrator's impression is one of exposure to a formidable collective mind. A sense of wonderment is evoked by their sheer animal otherness – something similar to what Melville's whale-men feel when they find themselves amid a school of whale mothers nursing their young.

It is notable that stepping outside the Western literary canon makes it easier to find a novel that engages directly with sheep as animals. Within the Western tradition of the visual arts, too, it can be difficult to find works featuring sheep that do not negate their animality by acceding to the overwhelmingly powerful associations bequeathed by Judaeo-Christianity and pastoral-ism. In European painting for the last several centuries, sheep have mostly been used to furnish a landscape, as part of a pas-toral or Arcadian scene. Where a sheep appears centre stage, it is usually either because it has been transformed into a symbol – the Lamb of God, the flock of the Good Shepherd – or because the painting's purpose is to record the inflated achievements of the stock-breeder.

Perhaps one difficulty peculiar to the visual arts, in depicting domestic sheep in and for themselves, is the creation of interest out of their apparent formlessness. More than any other animal, domestic sheep – especially the most common high-wool- and high-meat-yielding breeds – look like nothing in particular. The

Franz Marc,
The Sheep,
1913–14,
oil on canvas.

outline of their bodies approaches the simple curve of an oval or a round-cornered rectangle, into which the head and legs all but disappear. Within this outline, the wavy lines of the fleece occur in gentle curls, so that sheep often come to resemble clouds – the kind we describe as 'fleecy' – floating over the hillside, soon to evaporate or drift away. This impression is confirmed by their usual colour, a slightly dirty white. No wonder the sheep encountered by Don Quixote seemed to dissipate into the clouds of dust they raised. It is hard to invest such blank shapes with visual intensity, drama or mystery.

One of the few who succeeds in producing a mesmerizing effect from these otherwise unpromising qualities is the Spanish artist Francisco de Zurbarán. In *Agnus Dei* (*c.* 1635), Zurbarán follows his usual still-life technique. He takes a familiar object and

invests it with visual sanctity – with a kind of numinous aura –
by placing it on a dark shelf against a dark background, then
illuminating it with a pale light from beyond the frame. By this
means, he transforms a perfectly ordinary yearling merino ram
– an animal observable in its millions in seventeenth-century
Spain – into an enhaloed symbol of Christian self-sacrifice, an
emblem of the transfiguration of bodily matter into spiritual
essence. The vulnerable, quivering, struggling flesh, which the
viewer knows the real animal must possess, has been stilled. The
wool, which would be tough and greasy to the touch, has been
softened and purified. And, despite the (to human eyes) rather
mask-like impassivity of the ovine face, Zurbarán has somehow,
without abandoning naturalism, given this animal an expression of saintly resignation. The body, and the curls of wool,
achieve exactly that rounded shapelessness we associate with
clouds in the heavens. This animal looks as if he is about to
ascend into paradise, like Jesus after the resurrection. He has
become, as the title states, the Lamb of God.

And yet – the exaggerated roundness of this sheep, the billow-
ing contour of his upper outline, is not, in fact, natural at all; it is
produced by the fact that his legs are bound together, forcing his
spine into a curve. Actually, all the features that make this animal
such a pure expression of spiritual meaning – his stillness, his
expression of patient martyrdom and his exposure to the sancti-
fying light – depend on the ligature around his ankles. That detail
– which protrudes in the direction of the viewer, seemingly out of
the foreground plane, almost out of the canvas itself – reveals
how the spiritual meaning of the painting is held together. These
bound hooves return us to material reality. This is not, after all,
a picture of patient self-surrender, but of constrictive power. This
sheep is not going willingly to slaughter at all – if he were, no
bonds would be necessary. In reality, of course, no sheep has ever

gone willingly to slaughter: that's simply not something animals do, except in the human imagination.

Of course, it is most unlikely this perspective would have been part of Zurbarán's intentions. On the contrary, in painting *Agnus Dei,* he was no doubt hoping to create another of the fervently devotional religious works to which he dedicated his career. It is only the critical distance provided by our awareness of the history of human treatment of animals that allows Matthew Scully, for example, to use *Agnus Dei* as an evocative cover image for his 2002 book on animal exploitation.[16]

Contemporary artists are more likely to confront the viewer deliberately with the material reality of sheep and their bodily fates, and in doing so, to de-familiarize, challenge or mock the symbolic meanings that long attached to them. Damien Hirst's *God Alone Knows* (2007) might be thought to attempt something of this kind. In this work, the flayed carcasses of three sheep, each stretched out in a cruciform pose, are preserved in vats of formaldehyde. Obviously, here, familiar religious iconography – Christ, the Lamb of God, dying for our sins on the cross – is being deliberately juxtaposed with the material reality of the gruesome flayed and contorted sheep carcasses, which look like something a walker might stumble upon in a remote pasture. As a triptych, the piece recalls the image of Christ crucified between two thieves – but this adds a further iconoclastic layer of meaning: which is the Lamb of God? What makes one of these crucified beings divine and the other two merely dead animal bodies?

Another way of viewing this work, however, is to see it as the predictable product of a very marketable kind of shock value, which has come to be expected of artists within the world of high-end corporate and investment art. In this context, the effect produced by these real carcasses ends up further than ever

from the actual lives and deaths of the animals who supply the raw material. Notoriously, Hirst doesn't make artworks like this himself: he comes up with the concept and employs assistants to create the pieces. By means of this entrepreneurial paradigm, the three sheep in *God Alone Knows* have been sublimated, in the chemical sense of being transformed into vapour; they have been absorbed into the rarefied ozone of hype that comprises high-end postmodern capitalism. They are products of a designer brand labelled 'Damien Hirst'. The title of the work might even hint that the artist is having a joke at the viewer's expense (and the buyer's). It sounds like a quotation from the Bible (perhaps an echo of Job 28:23: 'God understands the way to [wisdom] and he alone knows where it dwells'), but it is actually from a story told about the poet Robert Browning. When asked by a friend to explain the meaning of one of his poems, Browning is said to have replied, 'when I wrote it only God and I knew – now, God alone knows!'[17]

Francisco de Zurbarán, *Agnus Dei*, oil on canvas, c. 1635.

A very similar strategy to Hirst's can, however, produce radically different effects when deployed in another medium and in another context. In 2006 the world's most powerful animal advocacy organization, People for the Ethical Treatment of Animals (PETA), mounted a campaign against various practices used by sheep farmers in Australia – in particular, live export and mulesing. PETA timed the campaign to coincide with Easter, and planned to put up billboards all over Sydney that displayed a provocative image by the well-known British graphic artist Ralph Steadman: a mutilated and agonized sheep nailed to a cross, accompanied by the tag line 'Have mercy on them: stop mulesing and live exports.' Although the tactic is similar to that of Hirst's *God Alone Knows* – the generation of shock by replacing the familiar image of Christ as the sacrificed Lamb of God with the image of a crucified animal – the differences are clear and vital. In Hirst's piece, the shock is created mostly by the use of a flayed animal carcass, and it remains preserved within the self-reflecting bubble of the art world, where such effects are expected, even required of artistic *enfants terribles*. Steadman's image, which does not use an actual animal's body, nor even depict its suffering realistically, but instead caricatures it, nevertheless creates a far more effective and wide-ranging provocation. This is for two reasons: because Steadman's image directly refers to and challenges the everyday human practices of farming and consumption that cause suffering; and because, as a billboard, it aims to do so in as public a sphere as possible. PETA's press releases emphasized this strategy:

> The lamb on a crucifix reminds us that these gentle animals are mutilated, tormented and killed every day in Australia for nothing more than very un-Christian greed ... If Christ were here, he would show mercy to these lambs, so we're asking the Australian government to follow his

compassionate example and bring an end to these two hideous abuses.[18]

The continued investment of contemporary cultures in maintaining the separation between these symbolic and material treatments of sheep is suggested by the fact that the image never went on public display, because no advertising company would agree to put it on billboards.

Maryrose Crook's startling and oblique *Lamb of Constant Sorrow* (2006) also depends on the juxtaposition of the sheep's symbolic meaning with its material fate – although in yet another different context. The painting depicts a leg of lamb, butcher-dressed, oven-ready – except that it is decorated with delicate crosses made of pearls, and emblazoned with a portrait of an extinct bird, which New Zealanders will recognize as the South Island kōkako (*Callaeas cinerea cinerea*). By displaying them on a bed of luxurious pink silk, surrounded by gem-like icons, the painting invites viewers to consider the hidden meaning that links these two dead animals, the recently extinct bird and the recently dispatched lamb. By general consensus the kōkako's song is the most beautiful of any New Zealand bird, and since one of its subspecies has recently been declared extinct while the other remains critically endangered, the bird represents the lost or severely threatened endemic natural beauty that remains one of New Zealand's standard defining features. On the other hand, the leg of lamb emblematizes the pastoral agriculture upon which modern New Zealand was founded, both economically and culturally. But bird and sheep are linked more closely than that. Because of their diet and habits, kōkako need large, unbroken areas of diverse forest. Unfortunately for them, large-scale sheep farming has always demanded the exact opposite: large, unbroken areas of monoculture pastureland. Forest clearance for pastoralism and the decline of endemic species are different sides of the same story;

overleaf:
Crucified Sheep, by the cartoonist Ralph Steadman, 2006, ink on paper.

Maryrose Crook, *Lamb of Constant Sorrow*, 2006, oil on canvas.

the extinction of one of the animals represented in Crook's painting is causally related to the life and death of the other.

These works by Hirst, Steadman and Crook all challenge their viewers, in different ways, to think about the series of transactions, both symbolic and material, by which humans and sheep interrelate. In that respect they are still, one way or another, less interested in engaging artistically with sheep as living animals in themselves, and more interested in problematizing the ways we think about and deal with them. There is, however, at least one major modern artist who has seen the gently curving shape of the woolly sheep as a form worthy of investigation in itself.

Henry Moore, one of the pre-eminent sculptors of the twentieth century, devoted an entire sketchbook to nearly 100 drawings of sheep. Art critic Kenneth Clark sums up the predictable sense of surprise that such a major artist should take an interest in sheep: 'what could the master of pure form find in the shapeless bodies of these woolly animals?' Moore answers the question both in the drawings themselves and in his account of how they came about. During preparations for a major exhibition of his work in Florence in 1972, he writes, 'the shippers and packers were all around, making such a disturbance that it was impossible to work, and I retired into a small studio which faces the field that I let to a local farmer for sheep grazing.' By doing so – enacting a kind of microcosm of the pastoral genre, a withdrawal from hectic modern life into the simpler verities of the rural estate – Moore achieved unexpected artistic refreshment:

These sheep often wandered up close to the window of the little studio I was working in. I began to be fascinated by them, and to draw them. At first I saw them as rather shapeless balls of wool with a head and four legs. Then I began to realize that underneath all that wool was body,

Henry Moore, 'Sheep with Lamb', from *Sheep Sketchbook* (1980).

which moved in its own way, and that each sheep had its individual character.

Moore recounts an artistic process that begins with an initial blindness to ovine form: he sees them initially as nebulous things, indistinguishable from one another, the same way most of us perceive sheep most of the time. But then, by means of close attention, he discovers the individual living beings obscured beneath his first dim and unfocused impression. This process requires a certain kind of cooperation from the animals themselves:

> If I tapped on the window the sheep would stop and look, with that sheepish stare of curiosity. They would stand like that for up to five minutes, and I could get them to hold the same pose for longer by just tapping again on the window. It wouldn't last as long the second time, but altogether the sheep posed as well as a life model in an art school.[19]

Henry Moore, *Sheep Piece*, 1971–2. 'I have always liked sheep,' Moore wrote, 'and there is one big sculpture of mine that I called *Sheep Piece* because I placed it in a field and the sheep enjoyed it and the lambs played around it.'

Henry Moore, 'Sheep Back View', from *Sheep Sketchbook* (1980).

Moore's unconventional association of sheepishness with curiosity – the mindful engagement of the animal with the human observer – shows how far his artistic process takes him away from the overwhelmingly dominant assumptions about sheep. Or conversely, perhaps, it shows how far his refusal to accept those assumptions allows him to advance in artistic terms.

The artworks above embody vividly one of the main questions motivating this book: what does it mean to try and look at sheep as they really are, rather than to remain content with seeing them as we have made them? Or, to put it another way, what would it mean to think about sheep in terms of their experience of sheepliness, rather than our own presupposition of their sheepishness?

I began my first chapter by recounting my visit to a farm sanctuary, where I had hoped to find out something about what sheep are really like, in themselves. Yet, as I described, that proved more difficult than I had anticipated. There I was, face to face with a sheep, meeting his gaze, yet finding it impossible to read his expression.

But then something happened to change that. A second sheep came up behind 'my' sheep and touched a nose to his rump, prompting him to turn and lay his chin over the dip in his companion's back. Now, suddenly, my sheep's body seemed full of meaning, animated by vital signs. In ovine terms, the chin-on-the-back gesture expresses what animal behaviourists call a 'bond'. Not that I needed science to tell me so: it was immediately obvious that here was an animal who was greeting a friend affectionately.

And isn't it natural, after all, that animals – especially animals like sheep – will express their characters more fully when they can turn away from us, and towards each other? Regarding humans, they are bound to be guarded and wary. Anyway, why should they care what they mean to us? It's what they mean to each other that matters to them.

Timeline of the Sheep

c. 2,500,000 BCE	c. 9000 BCE	c. 4000 BCE	c. 2000 BCE
Sheep and goats evolve in Eurasia	Earliest evidence of domestic sheep (in Mesopotamia)	Domestic sheep spread to British Isles and China, completing their expansion through Eurasia and North Africa	Earliest evidence of distinct (human-produced) breeds. Emergence of wool textile crafts

1493	1536–41	1667
Christopher Columbus introduces domestic sheep to the Americas	Dissolution of the monasteries and further enclosures under Henry VIII	Jean-Baptiste Denys and Richard Lower experiment with the transfusion of lambs' blood to human subjects

1792	1820s–40s	1882
'The Year of the Sheep': forced enclosures in the Scottish Highlands result in riots and forced exile for many Sir Joseph Banks establishes a flock of merinos at Kew for George III	Australia's 'Great Pastoral Age'	First shipment of frozen lamb from New Zealand to Britain

60 CE	711	1128	1363

De re rustica by Columella documents Roman pastoral practices

Conquest of Iberian Peninsula by North African Berbers and Arabs, who take their sheep breeds with them; likely origins of the merino

Cistercian Order arrives in England and begins to establish large monastic sheep farms

Establishment by the Norman kings of Calais of the 'Wool Staple', the central port for the wool trade, under English control

1760s	1770s	1788

Robert Bakewell develops the 'first modern breed of sheep', the New (or Dishley) Leicester

Richard Arkwright opens the first mechanized textile mills in the north of England

'First flock' arrives in Australia

5 July 1996	2000–2012	2001

Dolly the sheep born in Roslin Institute, Edinburgh

Half a million sheep die aboard Australian live export vessels

3.8 million stock animals slaughtered in Great Britain due to foot-and-mouth scare

References

1 SHEEPISHNESS

1 Henry David Thoreau, *Walden* [1854] (London, 1980), p. 206.
2 George Orwell, *Animal Farm* [1945] (London, 1995), pp. 39, 64–5, 129.
3 Aristotle, *The Natural History of Animals*, Book 9, part 3, online at The Internet Classics Archive, www.classics.mit.edu, accessed 23 April 2014.
4 Edward Topsell, *A History of Four-footed Beastes* (London, 1607), p. 601.
5 Georges-Louis Leclerc, Comte de Buffon, *Natural History: General and Particular*, vol. III (Edinburgh, 1780), Eighteenth Century Collections Online, www. quod.lib.umich.edu, pp. 462–6.
6 Lady Mary Anne Barker, *Station Amusements* (London, 1873), pp. 222 and 225.
7 Richard Barber, trans., *Bestiary* (Woodbridge, 1992), pp. 77–8.
8 Roel Sterckx, '"Of a Tawny Bull We Make Offering": Animals in Early Chinese Religion', in *A Communion of Subjects: Animals in Religion, Science and Ethics*, ed. Paul Waldau and Kimberley Patton (New York, 2006), pp. 265–6.
9 Patricia Bjaaland Welch, *Chinese Art: A Guide to Motifs and Visual Imagery* (Rutland, VT, 2008), pp. 130–31.
10 Ellen Meloy, *Eating Stone: Imagination and the Loss of the Wild* (New York, 2006), pp. 199–203.

1 'The Debate Between Sheep and Grain', The Electronic Text Corpus of Sumerian Literature, www.etcsl.orinst.ox.ac.uk, accessed 7 April 2014.

2 Rudyard Kipling, *Just So Stories for Little Children* (New York, 1902), pp. 197–224. Kipling here refers to an ancient divination practice whereby the shoulder blade of the sheep is thrown in the fire and then removed so the pattern of fractures produced by the flames can be read for oracles: see John and Caitlín Matthews, *The Element Encyclopedia of Magical Creatures* (London, 2005), p. 515.

3 M. L. Ryder, *Sheep and Man* (London, 1983), p. 4.

4 'Barbary Sheep', in *Animal*, ed. David Burnie (London, 2001), p. 256; Valerius Geist, *Mountain Sheep: A Study in Behavior and Evolution* (Chicago, IL, 1971), p. 3. Species classifications for *Ovis* remain very much in dispute. For example, some experts use *O. aries vignei* for the urial and *O. aries orientalis* for the mouflon; some use *O. musimon* for the mouflon; some regard the Dall and the Siberian bighorn as distinct species (*O. dalli* and *O. nivicola* respectively). The classifications used here follow Ryder, who gives what seem to be the simplest and clearest designations.

5 'Argali', in *Animal*, ed. Burnie, p. 256.

6 Marco Polo, *The Travels of Marco Polo*, trans. Ronald Latham (London, 1968), p. 63.

7 Geist, *Mountain Sheep*, pp. 4–8.

8 Ryder, *Sheep and Man*, pp. 14–15.

9 Bijal B. Trivedi, 'Scientists Clone First Endangered Animal: A Wild Sheep', *National Geographic Today* (29 October 2001), http://news.nationalgeographic.com, accessed 2 May 2014.

10 Geist, *Mountain Sheep*, p. 4.

11 Ryder, *Sheep and Man*, p. 3.

12 Of course, scientists themselves have been well aware of, and have tried to grapple with, the uncertainties and contradictions of the concept of species since at least the 1950s. See, for

example, J. R. Gregg, 'Taxonomy, Language and Reality', *American Naturalist*, LXXXIV/819 (November–December 1950), pp. 419–35.

13 Charles Darwin, *The Variation of Animals and Plants Under Domestication*, vol. I (London, 1875), p. 98.

14 J. C. Ewart, 'Domestic Sheep and their Wild Ancestors', *Transactions of the Highland and Agricultural Society of Scotland*, V/25 (1910), pp. 160–91.

15 Ryder, *Sheep and Man*, pp. 20–22.

16 Ibid., pp. 19–25.

17 Hannah Velten, *Cow* (London, 2007), pp. 19–21.

18 Ryder, *Sheep and Man*, p. 25.

19 Carl Sauer, *Agricultural Origins and Dispersals* (New York, 1952), pp. 85–6; Brett Mizelle, *Pig* (London, 2011), pp. 27–8.

20 Donna Haraway, *Primate Visions: Gender, Race and Nature in the World of Modern Science* (New York, 1989), pp. 187–212.

21 Ryder, *Sheep and Man*, p. 27.

22 Ibid., pp. 28–9.

23 Ibid., pp. 17, 31.

24 'Cattle and Relatives', in *Animal*, ed. Burnie, p. 244.

25 Ryder, *Sheep and Man*, p. 10.

26 'Cattle and Relatives', p. 244.

27 Ryder, *Sheep and Man*, pp. 5–6.

28 So-called wools from other animals, such as cashmere and mohair from goats and angora from rabbits, are actually types of hair, different from sheep's wool in their chemical makeup and properties.

29 Alan Butler, *Sheep: The Remarkable Story of the Humble Animal that Made the Modern World* (New York, 2006), pp. 11–12.

30 Ryder, *Sheep and Man*, p. 5.

31 Geist, *Mountain Sheep*, pp. 112, 131.

32 Ibid., pp. 177, 232, 235.

33 T. E. Rowell and C. A. Rowell, 'The Social Organization of Feral *Ovis aries* Ram Groups in the Pre-rut Period', *Ethology*, XCV (1993), pp. 213–32; pp. 230–31.

34 Geist describes how difficult he found it to overcome his reluctance to 'conceive of these magnificent beasts as queers' in *Mountain Sheep and Man in the Northern Wilds* (Ithaca, NY, 1975), pp. 97–8.

35 George B. Schaller, *Mountain Monarchs: Wild Sheep and Goats of the Himalaya* (Chicago, IL, 1977), p. 238.

36 Bruce Bagemihl, *Biological Exuberance: Animal Homosexuality and Natural Diversity* (New York, 1999), pp. 405–7. Animal scientists in the USA have been hard at work trying to identify homosexuality in sheep: 'the long-term goal was to determine the biological and genetic basis of homosexual behaviour, so that duds [the term investigators used for a ram sexually interested only in other rams] could be weeded out of domestic sheep, enhancing the economics of sheep raising'. See Joan Roughgarden, *Evolution's Rainbow: Diversity, Gender, and Sexuality in Nature and People* (Berkeley, CA, 2004), p. 139.

37 Theodosius Dobzhansky, 'Nothing in Biology Makes Sense Except in the Light of Evolution', *American Biology Teacher*, XXXV (1973), pp. 125–9. A recent example of Dawkins's use of the phrase can be found by entering the phrase as a search term on the website of the Richard Dawkins Foundation at www.richarddawkins.net.

38 Jonathan Balcombe, *The Pleasurable Kingdom: Animals and the Nature of Feeling Good* (Houndmills, 2006).

39 Bagemihl, *Biological Exuberance*, p. 253.

40 J. P. Scott, 'Social Behavior, Organization and Leadership in a Small Flock of Domestic Sheep', *Comparative Psychology Monographs*, XVIII/4 (February 1945), p. 4.

41 *Pliny's Natural History*, trans. and ed. Jonathan Couch et al. (London, 1847–8), vol. III, Book VIII, chap. 47, p. 86.

42 Scott, 'Social Behavior', pp. 8, 15–16, 24, 26.

43 Rowell and Rowell, 'Social Organization', p. 230.

44 Scott, 'Social Behavior', p. 24.

45 Sarah Franklin, *Dolly Mixtures: The Remaking of Genealogy* (Durham, NC, 2007), p. 200.

46 Mary Hunter Austin, *The Flock* (Boston, MA, 1906), p. 109.

47 Franklin, *Dolly Mixtures*, pp. 200–201.

48 Thomas Tryon, *The Country-Man's Companion* (London, 1688), p. 61.

49 Caroline Lee et al., 'Development of a Maze Test and its Application to Assess Spatial Learning and Memory in Merino Sheep', *Applied Animal Behaviour Science*, XCVI (2006), pp. 43–51.

50 Martin Wainwright, 'Pennine Spot Where Sheep Won't Be Fenced In', *The Guardian* (30 July 2004). I obtained confirmation of the veracity of this story from the daughter of Mrs Dorothy Lindley, who witnessed the behaviour and was quoted in the original reports: personal communication, 2 May 2014.

51 John Gray, 'Hefting onto Place: Intersecting Lives of Humans and Sheep on Scottish Hill Landscape', *Anthrozoös*, XXVII/2 (2014), pp. 219–34.

52 Geist, *Mountain Sheep*, pp. 133–4.

53 Rowell and Rowell, 'Social Organization', pp. 213, 241.

54 Keith M. Kendrick et al., 'Sheep Don't Forget a Face', *Nature*, CDXIV (8 November 2001), pp. 165–6.

55 Bijal P. Trivedi, 'Sheep are Highly Adept at Recognising Faces, Study Shows', *National Geographic News* (7 November 2001).

56 Other studies by the same team showed that the sheep were adept at reading the emotions of photographed faces: they preferred the images of contented sheep over stressed ones, and those of smiling humans over frowning ones. See Jonathan Balcombe, *The Exultant Ark: A Pictorial Tour of Animal Pleasure* (Berkeley, CA, 2011), p. 12.

3 ANCIENT YARNS

1 M. L. Ryder, *Sheep and Man* (London, 1983), pp. viii and 56. For similarly sweeping claims see Alan Butler, *Sheep: The Remarkable Story of the Humble Animal that Made the Modern World* (New York, 2006), p. vii, and Sarah Franklin, *Dolly Mixtures: The Remaking of Genealogy* (Durham, NC, 2007), p. 6.

2 'The Debate between Sheep and Grain', The Electronic Text Corpus of Sumerian Literature, www.etcsl.orinst.ox.ac.uk, accessed 7 April 2014.

3 Ryder, *Sheep and Man*, p. 50.

4 Ibid., pp. 28–9.

5 Ibid., p. 738.

6 Ibid., pp. 78, 96–7.

7 Alberto Manguel, *A History of Reading* (New York, 1996), p. 27.

8 Ryder, *Sheep and Man*, p. 106.

9 Ibid., pp. 17, 28–9, 31.

10 J. D. Pearson, 'A Mendelian Interpretation of Jacob's Sheep',
    Science and Christian Belief, XIII/1 (2001), pp. 51–8.

11 Robert Graves, *The Greek Myths* (London, 1960), vol. II, p. 529;
    Ryder, *Sheep and Man*, p. 147.

12 Felix Guirand, ed., *New Larousse Encyclopedia of Mythology*
    (London, 1968), p. 37.

13 Ryder, *Sheep and Man*, pp. 105–8.

14 Ibid., p. 94.

15 'The Code of Hammurabi', trans. L. W. King, online at the Avalon
    Project, www.avalon.law.yale.edu, accessed 14 April 2014.

16 Ryder, *Sheep and Man*, pp. 118–19, 125, 147.

17 Ibid., pp. 114–15.

18 The Roman poet Catullus, writing in the first century BCE, gives a
    technically detailed description of the Fates spinning the futures
    of the heroes of the Trojan war from a willow-basket full of
    'woolen fleeces, soft and shiny white'; see *The Complete Poetry of
    Catullus*, trans. David Mulroy (Madison, WI, 2002), Poem 64,
    lines 311–20, p. 68.

19 Ryder, *Sheep and Man*, p. 141.

20 Homer, *Iliad*, trans. Robert Fagles (London, 1996) Book 4, lines
    503–5, p. 82.

21 Ibid., Book 3, lines 150–53, p. 56.

22 Homer, *Odyssey*, trans. Robert Fagles (London, 1996), Book 24,
    lines 136–68, p. 425.

23 Ibid., Book 9, lines 469–526, pp. 160–62.

24 Walter O. Moeller, *The Wool Trade of Ancient Pompeii* (Leiden,
    1976), p. 4.

25 Ibid., p. 10.

26 Varro, *De re rustica*, trans. W. D. Hooper and H. B. Ash, online at LacusCurtius: Into the Roman World, www.penelope.uchicago.edu, accessed 15 April 2014, Book 2, section 1, 4–6, 20.

27 Ryder, *Sheep and Man*, pp. 194–5.

28 Ibid., pp. 198–9, 228–93, 418–25.

29 Ibid., pp. 210–13.

30 Ibid., pp. 120, 228–30.

31 Herodotus, *The Histories*, trans. Aubrey de Sélincourt (London, 2006), Book III, section 113, p. 198.

32 John Goodridge, 'The Case of John Dyer's Fat-tailed Sheep and their Tail-trolleys: "A Thing to Some Scarce Credible"', *Agricultural History Review*, LIV/2 (2006), pp. 229–39.

33 Ryder, *Sheep and Man*, pp. 120, 228–30.

34 Ibid., pp. 198–9, 228–93, 418–25.

4 A SHEEP-SHAPED WORLD

1 Modern experts tend to regard Herdwicks as closely related to other mountain sheep of Wales and the west of England: see Harriet Ritvo, 'Counting Sheep in the English Lake District: Rare Breeds, Local Knowledge, and Environmental History', in *Beastly Natures: Animals, Humans, and the Study of History*, ed. Dorothee Brantz (Charlottesville, VA, 2010), pp. 269–71.

2 M. L. Ryder, *Sheep and Man* (London, 1983), pp. 34–9, 185, 192–3.

3 Ibid., pp. 189–92, 444, 455.

4 Jonathan Sumption, *The Hundred Years' War: Trial by Battle* (Philadelphia, PA, 1991), pp. 41–2.

5 'Woolsack', www.parliament.uk, accessed 18 April 2014.

6 Sumption, *Hundred Years' War*, pp. 41–2.

7 Robert Trow-Smith, *A History of British Livestock Husbandry to 1700* (London, 1957), p. 139.

8 Richard Barber, trans., *Bestiary* (Woodbridge, 1992), pp. 77–81; Ryder, *Sheep and Man*, pp. 451–2.

9 Barber, *Bestiary*, pp. 80–81.

10 Alan Butler, *Sheep: The Remarkable Story of the Humble Animal that Made the Modern World* (New York, 2006), pp. 44–6.

11 Trow-Smith, *British Livestock Husbandry to 1700*, pp. 131–2.

12 Butler, *Sheep*, pp. 3–5; Ryder, *Sheep and Man*, pp. 450–52.

13 Butler, *Sheep*, pp. 43–4.

14 Thomas More, *Utopia*, trans. George M. Logan and Robert M. Adams (London, 2011), pp. 15–16.

15 Butler, *Sheep*, pp. 75–81.

16 Karl Marx, *Capital: A Critique of Political Economy*, trans. Samuel Moore and Edward Aveling (New York, 1906), vol. I, pp. 465–6.

17 Karl Marx, *Capital: A Critique of Political Economy*, trans. Ernest Moore Untermann (Chicago, IL, 1909), vol. III, p. 599.

18 Joyce E. Salisbury, *The Beast Within: Animals in the Middle Ages* (London, 1994), p. 24.

19 Keith Ponting, *Sheep of the World* (Poole, 1980), p. 16.

20 Eileen Power, *The Wool Trade in English Medieval History* (Oxford, 1941), p. 13.

21 Miguel de Cervantes, *Don Quixote de la Mancha*, trans. Tobias Smollett (London, 1995), pp. 104–7.

22 Ponting, *Sheep of the World*, p. 15.

23 Power, *Wool Trade*, p. 13.

24 Sarah Franklin, *Dolly Mixtures: The Remaking of Genealogy* (Durham, NC, 2007), pp. 97–9 and 219 n. 18.

25 Alfred Crosby, *Ecological Imperialism: The Biological Expansion of Europe, 900–1900* (Cambridge, 1986), p. 173.

26 Ryder, *Sheep and Man*, pp. 580–83.

27 Elinor G. K. Melville, *A Plague of Sheep: Environmental Consequences of the Conquest of Mexico* (Cambridge, 1997), pp. 4, 8, 51–2, 120, 154.

28 Barney Nelson, *The Wild and the Domestic: Animal Representation, Ecocriticism, and Western American Literature* (Reno, NV, 2000), p. 75.

29 John Prebble, *The Highland Clearances* (Harmondsworth, 1963), p. 28.

30 Franklin, *Dolly Mixtures*, p. 111.

31 Ibid., p. 119.

32 Ibid., p. 120.

33 Paul Edmund de Strzelecki, *Physical Description of New South Wales and Van Diemen's Land* (London, 1841), pp. 366–77.

34 James Collier, *The Pastoral Age in Australia* (London, 1911), pp. 4–6.

35 Franklin, *Dolly Mixtures*, p. 118.

36 Ibid., pp. 138–49; see also Ryder, *Sheep and Man*, pp. 611–20.

37 James Belich, *Making Peoples: A History of the New Zealanders from Polynesian Settlement to the End of the Nineteenth Century* (Auckland, 1996), pp. 341–3.

38 Hugh Stringleman and Robert Peden, 'Sheep Farming', *Te Ara: The Encyclopedia of New Zealand*, www.teara.govt.nz, accessed 6 May 2014.

39 Thomas Hardy, *Far from the Madding Crowd* (London, 1985), pp. 41, 146–8, 407.

40 H. Guthrie-Smith, *Tutira: The Story of a New Zealand Sheep Station* (Wellington, 1969), p. 135.

41 Samuel Butler, *Erewhon: or, Over the Range* (London, 1920), p. 3.

42 James Belich, *The New Zealand Wars and the Victorian Interpretation of Racial Conflict* (Auckland, 1986).

43 James Belich, *Paradise Reforged: A History of the New Zealanders from the 1880s to the Year 2000* (Auckland, 2001), pp. 53–75.

44 Stringleman and Peden, 'Sheep Farming'.

45 Guthrie-Smith, *Tutira*, p. 142.

46 Ibid., pp. 179, 191–3.

47 Ibid., pp. 204, 325. For a revealing account of Guthrie-Smith's revisions to the various editions of *Tutira*, see Alex Calder, *The Settler's Plot: How Stories Take Place in New Zealand* (Auckland, 2012), pp. 140–43.

48 Guthrie-Smith, *Tutira*, p. XIII.

5 LITTLE LAMB, WHO MADE THEE?

1 Daniel Defoe, *A Tour through the Whole Island of Great Britain*, vol. III (London, 1778), pp. 153–4; the sentence in square brackets comprises a footnote in the original text.

2 Ibid., pp. 155–6.
3 Alan Butler, *Sheep: The Remarkable Story of the Humble Animal that Made the Modern World* (New York, 2006), pp. 106–7. The account of the emergence of automated mills in the next few paragraphs is also drawn from Butler, pp. 105–14.
4 William Youatt, *Sheep: The Breeds, Management, and Diseases* (London, 1837), pp. iii–iv.
5 Jonathan Swift, *Gulliver's Travels* (New York, 2002), p. 154.
6 In 1999, agricultural research scientists in New Zealand gave serious consideration to a project designed to develop 'the Peerless Shearless' – a 'wool-less meat sheep' produced through genetic engineering. The project did not go ahead. See 'Greens Welcome Backtrack on GE Sheep-without-wool', New Zealand Green Party press release (15 November 1999), www.greens.org.nz, accessed 13 May 2014.
7 Sarah Franklin, *Dolly Mixtures: The Remaking of Genealogy* (Durham, NC, 2007), pp. 83, 102.
8 Robert Trow-Smith, *A History of British Livestock Husbandry, 1700–900* (London, 1959), p. 60.
9 Roger J. Wood and Vítězslav Orel, *Genetic History in Selective Breeding: A Prelude to Mendel* (Oxford, 2001), p. 95; cited in Franklin, *Dolly Mixtures*, p. 95.
10 Thomas Bewick, *A General History of Quadrupeds* (London, 1970), p. 64.
11 Ibid., pp. 61–2.
12 Ibid., pp. 60–61.
13 Arthur MacGregor, *Animal Encounters: Human and Animal Interaction in Britain from the Norman Conquest to World War I* (London, 2012), p. 433.
14 William Blake, 'The Lamb', in *William Blake: The Complete Illuminated Books* (London, 2000), p. 406.
15 William Blake, 'The Tyger', in *Complete Illuminated Books*, p. 409.
16 William Blake, 'Jerusalem', in *Complete Illuminated Books*, pp. 312, 451.

17 Catherine Amey, *Clean, Green and Cruelty-free? The True Story of Animals in New Zealand* (Wellington, 2008), pp. 23–4.

18 Ibid., p. 24; Michael Morris, 'Ethical Issues Associated with Sheep Fly Strike Research, Prevention and Control', www.sic.shibaura-it.ac.jp, accessed 24 March 2014, p. 24; Animals Australia, 'Mulesing', www.animalsaustralia.org, accessed 24 April 2014.

19 D. J. Mellor and K. J. Stafford, 'Acute Castration and/or Tailing Distress, and its Alleviation in Lambs', *New Zealand Veterinary Journal*, XLVIII (2000), pp. 33–43.

20 Amey, *Clean, Green and Cruelty-free*, pp. 54–5.

21 Australian Government Department of Agriculture, 'Livestock Mortalities for Exports by Sea', www.daff.gov.au, accessed 25 April 2014.

22 Animals Australia, 'Live Export Animal Welfare On-board: High Mortalities and Rejections – 30 Years of Evidence', www.banliveexport.com, accessed 25 April 2014.

23 Animals Australia, 'Live Export – the Facts', www.banliveexport.com, accessed 25 April 2014; 'New Footage Reveals Full Horror of Pakistan Sheep Cull', www.animalsaustralia. org, accessed 25 April 2014.

24 Franklin, *Dolly Mixtures*, pp. 164–6.

25 Ibid, pp. 161, 173–5; emphasis in original.

26 Pauline Cameron and Katie Kemsley, 'Sheep – Lamb', Vintage Fashion Guild, www.vintagefashionguild.org, accessed 30 April 2014.

27 Elisa Bob, 'Excuse Me, Ma'am, Are You Wearing Fetal Lamb?', Animals' Agenda, www.animalsagenda.org, accessed 30 April 2014.

28 *National Animal Ethics Advisory Committee Annual Report 1 January to 31 December 2012*, www.biosecurity.govt.nz, accessed 27 April 2014.

29 Humane Research Australia, 'Statistics: Animal Use in Research and Teaching', www.humaneresearch.org.au, accessed 26 April 2014.

30 Michael Morris, 'Ethical Issues'; Amey, *Clean, Green and Cruelty-free?*, pp. 106–7.

31 Kim A. Janatpour and Paul V. Holland, 'A Brief History of Blood Transfusion', in *Blood Banking and Transfusion Medicine* (Philadelphia, PA, 2007), p. 3.

32 Thomas Shadwell, *The Virtuoso*, ed. Marjorie Hope Nicolson and David Stuart Rodes (Lincoln, NE, 1966), p. 51.

33 Humane Research Australia, 'Case Studies: Farm Animals', www.humaneresearch.org.au, accessed 26 April 2014.

34 BBC News, 'Dolly the Sheep Clone Dies Young', www.news.bbc.co.uk, accessed 26 April 2014.

35 Ian Wilmut, Keith Campbell and Colin Tudge, *The Second Creation: Dolly and the Age of Biological Control* (Cambridge, MA, 2000), pp. 209–10.

36 Cited in Franklin, *Dolly Mixtures*, p. 160.

37 Wilmut et al., *The Second Creation*, pp. 3–5.

38 Franklin, *Dolly Mixtures*, p. 43.

6 SHEEPLINESS

1 John and Caitlín Matthews, *The Element Encyclopedia of Magical Creatures* (London, 2005), p. 515.

2 Sir John Mandeville, *Mandeville's Travels*, ed. M. C. Seymour (Oxford, 1968), p. 204.

3 Henry Lee, *The Vegetable Lamb of Tartary: A Curious Fable of the Cotton Plant* (London, 1887), pp. 6–8.

4 Erasmus Darwin, *The Botanic Garden*, 2 vols (London, 1825), vol. II, p. 145.

5 Lee, *Vegetable Lamb*, p. 46, citing Herodotus, *The Histories*, Book III, para. 106.

6 Alec Lindsay Poole, 'Vegetable Sheep', *Te Ara: Encyclopedia of New Zealand*, www.teara.govt.nz, accessed 7 May 2014.

7 John R. Jackson, 'The Vegetable Sheep of New Zealand', *Intellectual Observer*, XI (1967).

8 In fact, as the OED notes, the word 'maverick' itself originally referred to an unbranded free-ranging animal; it derives from the surname of Samuel Maverick, a

nineteenth-century Texas cattleman infamous for leaving his herds unbranded.

9   *Eating Media Lunch*, Paul Casserley et al. (Wellington, 8 June 2004).
10 Samuel Beckett, *Molloy, Malone Dies, The Unnamable* (New York, 1997), pp. 27–9, 179–81; Janet Frame, 'Two Sheep', in *Snowman Snowman* (New York, 1963), pp. 177–82; *Intensive Care* (New York, 1971), pp. 41–2.
11 Herman Melville, *Moby-Dick; or, The Whale* (Berkeley, CA, 1979), p. 189; Haruki Murakami, *A Wild Sheep Chase*, trans. Alfred Birnbaum (London, 2003), pp. 176, 283.
12 Murakami, *A Wild Sheep Chase*, p. 118.
13 Ibid., pp. 110–11.
14 Ibid., pp. 219–20.
15 F. J. Ollivier et al., 'Comparative Morphology of the Tapetum Lucidum (Among Selected Species)', *Veterinary Ophthalmology*, VII/1 (January–February 2004), pp. 11–22.
16 Matthew Scully, *Dominion: The Power of Man, the Suffering of Animals, and the Call to Mercy* (New York, 2002).
17 *The Speaker*, 3 May 1890, p. 492.
18 'Crucified Lamb Ad Not Allowed', *Sydney Morning Herald*, 14 April 2006, www.smh.com.au.
19 Henry Moore and Kenneth Clark, *Henry Moore's Sheep Sketchbook* (London, 1980).

Select Bibliography

Anon., 'The Debate Between Sheep and Grain', The Electronic Text
    Corpus of Sumerian Literature, www.etcsl.orinst.ox.ac.uk
Austin, Mary Hunter, *The Flock* (Boston, MA, 1906)
Butler, Alan, *Sheep: The Remarkable Story of the Humble Animal that
    Made the Modern World* (New York, 2006)
Coe, Sue, *Sheep of Fools* (Seattle, WA, 2006)
Ewart, J. C., 'Domestic Sheep and their Wild Ancestors', *Transactions
    of the Highland and Agricultural Society of Scotland*, V/25,
    pp. 160–91
Franklin, Sarah, *Dolly Mixtures: The Remaking of Genealogy*
    (Durham, NC, 2007)
Geist, Valerius, *Mountain Sheep: A Study in Behavior and Evolution*
    (Chicago, IL, 1971)
Guthrie-Smith, H., *Tutira: The Story of a New Zealand Sheep Station*
    (Wellington, 1969)
Hardy, Thomas, *Far from the Madding Crowd* (London, 1985)
Meloy, Ellen, *Eating Stone: Imagination and the Loss of the Wild*
    (New York, 2006)
Melville, Elinor G. K., *A Plague of Sheep: Environmental Consequences
    of the Conquest of Mexico* (Cambridge, 1997)
Moore, Henry, and Kenneth Clark, *Henry Moore's Sheep Sketchbook*
    (London, 1980)
Murakami, Haruki, *A Wild Sheep Chase*, trans. Alfred Birnbaum
    (London, 2003)
Ponting, Keith, *Sheep of the World* (Poole, 1980)

Power, Eileen, *The Wool Trade in English Medieval History*
    (Oxford, 1941)
Rowell, T. E., and C. A. Rowell, 'The Social Organization of Feral
    Ovis aries Ram Groups in the Pre-rut Period', *Ethology*, xcv (1993),
    pp. 213–32
Ryder, M. L., *Sheep and Man* (London, 1983)
Schaller, George B., *Mountain Monarchs: Wild Sheep and Goats of the*
    Himalaya (Chicago, il, 1977)
Scott, J. P., 'Social Behavior, Organization and Leadership in a Small
    Flock of Domestic Sheep', *Comparative Psychology Monographs*,
    xviii/4 (February 1945), pp. 1–29
Spenser, Edmund, *The Shepheard's Calendar* (1579), Renascence
    Editions, www.luminarium.org
Swann, Leonie, *Three Bags Full: A Sheep Detective Story*, trans. Anthea
    Bell (New York, 2008)
Thorpe, Leonie, *The Sheep on the Fourth Floor* (London, 2010)
Trow-Smith, Robert, *A History of British Livestock Husbandry to 1700*
    (London, 1957)
—, *A History of British Livestock Husbandry, 1700–1900* (London, 1959)
Tryon, Thomas, *The Country-man's Companion* (London, 1688)

Associations and Websites

National Bighorn Sheep Association (USA)
www.bighorn.com

National Sheep Association (UK)
www.nationalsheep.org.uk

Sheep 101
www.sheep101.info

Think Differently About Sheep
www.think-differently-about-sheep.com

SANCTUARIES

Black Sheep Sanctuary (New Zealand)
www.theblacksheep.org.nz

The Farm Animal Sanctuary (UK)
www.thefarmanimalsanctuary.co.uk

The Farm Animal Sanctuary (USA)
www.farmsanctuary.org

Fleecehaven Sheep Sanctuary (UK)
www.fleecehaven.org.uk

Little Oak Sanctuary (Australia)
www.littleoaksanctuary.org

Woodstock Farm Animal Sanctuary (USA)
www.woodstocksanctuary.org

ADVOCACY

Animals Australia
www.animalsaustralia.org/investigations/live-export

PETA
www.peta.org/issues/animals-used-for-clothing/wool-industry

Acknowledgements

In writing this book I have been amazed by the richness and diversity of facts, ideas, stories and art associated with sheep, and I'm profoundly grateful to the many people whose work and generosity have enabled me to reflect some portion of this wealth of material. My special thanks go to Lena Areskog, Jonathan Burt, Jennifer Clement, Sue Coe, Maryrose Crook, Wanda Embar, Anne Galloway, Douglas Horrell, Gregor Kregar, Maggie Land Blanck, Donald MacDonald-Ross, Roger Makepeace, Jo-Anne McArthur, the Henry Moore Foundation, Michael Morris, Jacob Ochieng' Konyango, Patrick O'Sullivan, Chris Riddell, Angela Singer and Ralph Steadman. As always, my greatest debt is to Annie Potts, without whose inspiration, assistance and love I certainly would never have written this book.

Photo Acknowledgements

The author and publishers wish to express their thanks to the below sources of illustrative material and / or permission to reproduce it. Every effort has been made to contact unacknowledged copyright holders. Any copyright holders we have been unable to reach or to whom inaccurate acknowledgements have been made please contact Reaktion Books, and corrections will be made in any subsequent printing.

AP Photo/Andres Kudacki: p. 76; Lena Areskog: pp. 36, 44, 49, 52; photo Philip Armstrong: p. 6; postcard collection of the author: p. 8; Bigstock.com: p. 25 (Eugene Sergeev), p. 26 (Vrabelpeter1), p. 39 (Al Parker), p. 41 (duallogic), p. 62 (Life on White), p. 80 (Septemberlegs); from the collection of Maggie Land Blanck: p. 113; Bodleian Library, University of Oxford: pp. 85, 87; courtesy of the artist (Sue Coe): pp. 131, 132; courtesy of the artist (Maryrose Crook): p. 167; courtesy of Wanda Embar: p. 50; The J. Paul Getty Museum, Los Angeles (digital image courtesy of the Getty's Open Content Program): p. 18; courtesy of the artist (Gregor Kregar): pp. 142, 143; Michael Leaman: p. 145; Lincolnshire County Council – Museum of Lincolnshire Life: p. 121; Roger Makepeace: p. 149; The Metropolitan Museum of Art: pp. 27 (Rogers Fund, 1924), 57 (purchase, James N. Spear Gift, 1981), 69 (gift of Norbert Schimmel Trust, 1989); Jo-Anne McArthur: pp. 134, 135, 137; courtesy of McDonald Institute for Archaeological Research, Cambridge: p. 60; Donald MacDonald-Ross: p. 96; reproduced by permission of the Henry Moore Foundation: pp. 169, 170, 171; New Zealand Film Commission: p. 153;

Index